JESUS:

Meet Him Again for the First Time

JESUS:

Meet Him Again for the First Time

By Paul Smith

Vision House Publishing, Inc.
Gresham, Oregon

JESUS: MEET HIM AGAIN FOR THE FIRST TIME
© 1994 by Vision House Publishing, Inc.

Published by Vision House Publishing, Inc.
1217 NE Burnside, Suite 403
Gresham, Oregon 97030

Printed in the United States of America.

"too much to ask"
Reprinted from *Polishing the Petoskey Stone,* © 1990 by Luci Shaw. Used by permission of Harold Shaw Publishers, Wheaton, IL.

Unless otherwise indicated, all Scripture references are from the Revised Standard Version of the Bible, © 1946, 1952, 1971, 1973, Division of Christian Education, National Council of the Churches of Christ in the USA.

94 95 96 97 98 99 00 01 02 03 — 10 9 8 7 6 5 4 3 2 1

Contents

Foreword

W hen one looks for a job, one has to accept the territory that goes with it. But when retirement looms, the choice is wide: East coast? West coast? Mountains or plains?

Margaret and I prayed about it and then chose Seattle for its mountains and the sea, as well as for family reasons. We love it here.

Now, seven years later, when people suggest there might be a better location or a better home somewhere else, we find our priorities have changed. We insist only that it must be close to West Side Presbyterian Church.

It is not that we would be unable to worship God in a Baptist church or as Episcopalians. It is simply that for seven years God has spoken to us through Pastor Paul Smith and through the Christian fellowship that the Holy Spirit has fashioned in the church, in response (at least in part) to our pastor and his teaching.

I do a bit of preaching myself, and have heard and appreciated many pastors and preachers in many great churches worldwide. But I have never before experienced the consistent sense, Sunday by Sunday, as I enter God's house, that I know He will speak to me today. Nor have I felt the need before, as I leave, to ask for a transcript or a tape of the sermon that has moved me. We send these tapes to our friends in India as well as to our own families, so that they, too, can experience the faithful interpretation of God's Word revealed to pastor Paul by the Holy Spirit, and fearlessly spoken out to all of us at West Side.

For seven years or so we were content merely to enjoy the freshness and the challenge of a great preacher, sharing him only with those to whom we sent our tapes. Finally it became even more clear that what we had was very special and could not be kept to ourselves. We joined those who began to nudge our pastor to speak to a wider audience by publishing his work in book form.

The title Paul has chosen, *Jesus: Meet Him Again for the First Time,* says exactly what you will be doing when you read this book.

This is true for several reasons. One is that Paul Smith is an artist with words. As each chapter unfolds you will see Jesus from a fresh perspective. The landscape of Nazareth and of Galilee become three-dimensional with bold and vivid colors. People walk out of the canvas of history, and live again. The truths of Scripture have been painstakingly researched along with contemporary history, and then boldly and beautifully simplified for our delight.

You will also love these chapters because of their relevance to our situation today. I sometimes enjoy reading the meditations of holy men of God who have lived and studied in monastic seclusion. They sometimes carry us up into mystical and almost heavenly places. Then one comes back, almost as from a dream, and wonders how this fits the pattern of our lives. Not Paul Smith! He is the father of four teenaged children. No monastic seclusion for him! His mind may explore the heavenly places, but his feet are on the ground.

I only wish this book had room for the children's addresses that Paul and all of us in church enjoy each Sunday. The little ones love him and feel free to shout the answers to his questions and even finish his sentences for him.

Paul is married to Carreen, who was his fellow student and fellow member of the choir at Wheaton College. As partners in service, in teaching, and in singing and as examples of parenting love, they have led their own lively brood of children in a way that is itself a living sermon. That also keeps Paul's public sermons right up to date and down to earth. He has a way of translating the immediacy of the day-to-day life of Jesus into the immediacy of the problems and solutions that face all of us today.

Once you start to read this book, you may find it difficult to put it down. Yet I think it might be a mistake to read it straight through. Each chapter grew out of a whole thoughtful and thought-provoking sermon. Few of us have either the memory or the spiritual digestion to eat twenty meals at one sitting, however attractive and well-cooked they might be. On the other hand, neither should this book be laid down in a random place or back on a shelf for a later chance encounter. Most of us are too busy to remember books exiled to shelf limbo.

This is the kind of book for the planned quiet time that each of us needs every day. My wife and I sit together in our personal devotions, morning and evening. One of those times always centers on a Bible reading and notes. The other is always the reading of a chapter or short segment of a book. Currently it is a book of very condensed Christian biographies, each chosen to bring out some feature that may be worth imitating. I suggest that *this* book would make a great basis for daily personal devotions, or perhaps for Saturdays and Sundays when there may be more time for meditation. In either case, it should be regular and planned.

Before I sat down to write this foreword, I already had heard most of these sermons. Yet I felt I should remind myself of what they said and see whether the written form communicated as well as when spoken from that platform of authority, the battlements of the pulpit.

I couldn't put it down! The themes stay fresh, and you cannot help but be blessed. It is with great pleasure, therefore, that I invite you to join Paul Smith as he encourages you to meet Jesus again . . . for the first time.

Dr. Paul Brand
Co-author, *Pain: The Gift Nobody Wants*

Introduction

I would like to invite you to walk with me through the tiny nation of Palestine and to witness the life of the most astonishing man in all of history. We will see the remarkable events which surrounded His birth, follow Him through childhood, and watch Him emerge as a young man, toned and prepared by His experiences to launch an incredible ministry. We will watch with increasing awe as He heals the sick, stills storms, walks on water, and even raises people from the dead! We will listen in amazement to the wisdom and authority of His teaching, though He was a young man with little education or experience. We will trace the steps by which His followers came to believe that He was in fact the long-awaited Messiah, the very Son of God. We will grieve with His disciples over His clashes with the authorities which ultimately resulted in His death by crucifixion. And then we will look on in awe as He appears to them on a number of occasions in a glorious, resurrected body, and feel with them a cautious optimism growing into an irrepressible celebration of His victory over death!

Our guides for this journey will be the very people whose lives were so radically reshaped by their encounter with this man. They will tell us firsthand what they saw, and what they thought. They will confess their skepticism no more reluctantly than they admit their deepening convictions.

They have impressed me—these honest, thoughtful, observant men and women who thought they could live their lives in comfortable obscurity but found themselves unceremoniously thrust onto the stage of history. They were very ordinary people, not unlike you and me, people living normal lives until, quite unexpectedly, they found themselves in the middle of the most significant events ever to confront the human race. It is no wonder they were bewildered at first. So would we have been. They were not gullible, credulous people, easy to deceive. Quite the contrary! They often frustrated Jesus with their reluctance to be convinced. Even after His resurrection they could not quite bring themselves to believe. It seemed wishful thinking to them. So they doubted their own eyes when He appeared and even shared a meal with them. They confessed honestly that He looked different when they saw Him after the crucifixion, as I am sure He did. His new body was in its ideal form, no longer trammeled by the abuse He had received.

But up close they could see His identifying scars, hear His reassuring voice, and look into His familiar eyes. They could feel His irresistible compassion for them. In the end they had no option but to believe. And their absolute conviction became a compelling testimony for all future generations.

This book is intended to bring their accounts together and allow them to introduce us to Jesus in a fresh way, just as they came to know Him. My hope is that you will listen to their stories with an open mind, as if you were hearing it for the first time. It is not impossible that God should visit this planet. And what a wonderful thing it would be if He did! Could this man Jesus actually be "the exact representation" of the Living God? Could He be the One in whom "all the fullness of God dwells bodily"? In the end only He can convince you. So I invite you to meet Him again . . . for the first time!

A People Prepared

(Luke 1:5-22; Malachi 3:1-4, 4:5-6)

There is, I think, a sixth sense one has about the approach of dawn. During the long night hours the world retreats fitfully into sleep, like a cat stirring, stretching, shifting positions, until the day's distractions recede and one is overtaken by a deep, inanimate slumber into which even dreams do not intrude. Only the stars stay awake during these hours, but they are quiet, or at least their silvery voices lie beyond the range of human ears.

But just before dawn there is a slight, almost imperceptible stirring. It is as if God has breathed on this, the jewel of His creation. It is not enough to stir the grass; in fact, one cannot really feel it at all. It is only a sensation of life or motion, the caress of a thought passing along the surface of the good earth, as if God is taking inventory of His prized possessions.

The birds seem to notice first, but they are quick to pass the word along. And soon there is a light shimmering of sound which seems to be reflected in the eastern sky by the faintest luminescence. Dawn has arrived!

As that moment arrived in Jerusalem, that first moment of dawn, every day for nearly a thousand years, excepting only one generation lived out in captivity, the priest watching for it from the highest pinnacle of the temple would give the signal to his companions waiting below and a three-fold blast from the silver trumpets would pierce the cool, crisp morning air, echoing across the Tyropoeon Valley and up the slopes of the Upper City, rolling through the marketplace and across the hills which stand sentinel around the Holy City.

It was the call to begin the day, from the first waking moment, with the Lord who had established His people here in Zion. Already certain priests, Levites, and sundry temple workers had gathered by the fitful red light that glowed on the altar of burnt offering to wash and prepare themselves for duty. Now by torch-light they divided into two parties to inspect the temple courts and meet again at the Hall of Hewn Polished Stones. Responsibilities for preparing the morning sacrifice, trimming the golden candlestick, and making ready the altar of incense within the Holy Place were assigned by lot.

As morning broke, the great gates of the temple were swung open to admit the worshipers. The lamb was once again examined to determine its fitness for the morning sacrifice, then watered from the golden bowl and laid in mystic fashion on the north side of the altar with its face to the west, as tradition described the binding of Isaac. Faithful worshipers gathered in their respective courts as the priest who was to administer the sacrifice took his place on the east side of the altar, toward the rising sun. It was time, as the day began, to acknowledge the inevitable cost of the sins of the people.

Still to come, however, was the most solemn part of the day's service. Another priest, chosen by lot, would enter the Holy Place to stand before the veil within the temple and offer up prayers for the people as a cloud of incense rose from the golden altar. To stand thus before God was a fearful and wonderful thing, a privilege offered a priest only once in a lifetime, if at all. And if he trembled in the presence of God, he felt as well the honor of standing as mediator between God and His people.

On this particular morning, in early October of the sixth year before our present era, the lot fell to a certain humble priest named Zechariah who was on duty that week with his division, the division of Abijah. Every priest was assigned to a particular division which was called up twice a year for a week of service at the temple. Zechariah, who was married to the daughter of a priest and thus doubly blessed, also carried a deep, personal sorrow—he and his wife Elizabeth had been unable to bear a child. Now they had become elderly, and the possibility of preserving their name into the next generation, an immeasurable honor for a Jew, had seemingly escaped them.

This morning, however, it is doubtful Zechariah was giving much thought to his wife's barrenness. He was an upright and godly person, as was his wife, and theirs was a private disappointment. But today for the first and last time in his life, the lot had fallen to him to enter the Holy Place and offer up incense and prayer on behalf of his people. How often during his three or four decades of service must he have imagined how it would be to fill this central role in worship for the nation of Israel.

When the moment arrived, Zechariah took the golden censer in his hands and, with two assistants, entered the Holy Place through the awesome partition which separated it from the Court of the Priests. Once inside, the first assistant reverently removed from the altar the remains of the previous evening's sacrifice and retired, backwards, from the temple. Then the second stepped forward with live coals taken from the altar of burnt offerings and spread them on the altar before withdrawing also in an attitude of humble reverence and worship. Now the old priest was alone in the Holy Place, his face lit only by the glow from the seven-branched candlestick. Before him, across the great hall, was the heavy veil which hung before the Holy of Holies. In centuries past, the Ark of the Covenant had rested there, marking God's presence in the midst of His people. Even today it was in this place that God's heart beat in the midst of Israel.

Outside the temple, the people and priests were prostrate in prayer as Zechariah walked slowly forward, past the great candelabra on his left and the table of shewbread on his right, up the long passage, seemingly into the very presence of God. At last he stood before the altar, on which he placed the incense and stepped back to offer up the prayers on behalf of his people. He would likely have recalled times of deliverance from the past, sought God's blessings upon his people for the present, and entreated the Lord concerning the future of Israel. As the incense ignited, a great, aromatic cloud lifted heavenward, bearing with it his prayers on behalf of his nation.

Now Zechariah began to move reverently away from the altar. He must not delay here, lest some impure thought or motive betray him to a holy God. But suddenly, as he stepped back from that sacred spot, Zechariah saw, standing between the candlestick and the altar, a form which he recognized immediately to be an angel of the Lord. He had appeared from nowhere and his countenance was unmistakable. Zechariah was terrified. Never before had an angel appeared to a common priest in the temple, though the fear of encountering some divine apparition was never absent from those who undertook the sacrifices. The old priest's face no doubt blanched and his eyes widened as he started backwards.

"Do not be afraid, Zechariah," the angel said, "your prayer has been heard." His mind must have raced to recall his words and be certain that he had said the right thing before the Lord. Had he been aware enough that God was listening to his prayers? But now the angel said a most unexpected thing. "Your wife Elizabeth will bear you a son, and you are to give him the name John," which Zechariah knew to mean "God is gracious."

"He will be a joy and delight to you, and many will rejoice because of his birth, for he will be great in the sight of the Lord."

This was astonishing. Zechariah, I think, had been quite unconscious of himself in this holy place. He would have focused his attention on his symbolic role for this once-in-a-lifetime experience as mediator for his people before the Lord. But now, here was an angel from the Lord telling him that God was going to give him and his wife a personal blessing. Soon he would discover that the answer to his personal prayers and his prayers on behalf of the nation were being answered together in one mighty act of God.

"He is never to take wine or other fermented drink," the angel went on, describing the Nazirite vow with which Zechariah would have been quite familiar, "and he will be filled with the Holy Spirit even from birth." It was coming too fast. He and his beloved wife had longed and prayed for a child for so many years, it was almost a fading memory. The angel had said that Elizabeth, his own wife, would bear a son. But what was the angel saying about this child? He would be great in the sight of the Lord, and they were to see that he fulfilled the Nazirite vow, and God's Spirit would fill him even from birth. What did God have in mind?

"Many of the people of Israel will he bring back to the Lord their God," the angel continued.

And he will go on before the Lord, in the spirit and power of Elijah, to turn the hearts of the fathers to their children and the disobedient to the wisdom of the righteous—to make ready a people prepared for the Lord.

The words began to sound familiar. Zechariah, the godly priest, had read them many times in the Holy Scriptures. Always among the prophets there was this image of the great prophet Elijah preparing the way for the promised Messiah. In fact, the final words of the prophet Malachi (as God's revelation had ended some 400 years earlier) were:

Behold, I will send you Elijah the prophet before the great and terrible day of the LORD comes. And he will turn the hearts of fathers to their children and the hearts of children to their fathers, lest I come and smite the land with a curse (Malachi 4:5-6).

Slowly it must have dawned upon him that the God who had been silent for some four centuries was now beginning to speak. What was it the prophet Malachi had said? "Behold, I send my messenger to prepare the way before me, and the Lord whom you seek will suddenly come to his temple." Could it be that the promised Messiah was about to come to His temple? Surely Zechariah, for one, had always believed it. But to believe it would happen some day, and to be present for the event itself, were two different things!

More than that—much more than that—the angel seemed to be saying that his own son, the child of his barren wife Elizabeth, would be the messenger who was to prepare the way for the Lord. This was more than he could fathom. "How can I be sure of this?" he asked in his bewilderment and confusion. "I am an old man and my wife is well along in years." I don't believe Zechariah really doubted God's ability to do such a thing. It was just that to "believe" something and to anticipate it without question were quite different propositions. Most of us who "believe" Christ will return some day will likely be astonished beyond speech when He actually does appear.

In any case, the angel drew him up short. "I am Gabriel." Zechariah knew the name perfectly well. The great prophet Daniel, so many centuries before, had encountered Gabriel. "I stand in the presence of God," the angel said with compelling authority, "and I have been sent to speak to you and to tell you this good news. And now you will be silent and not able to speak until the day this happens, because you did not believe my words, which will come true at their proper time."

I think Zechariah became a believer on the spot! It would never again occur to him to question the possibility of anything the Lord said. Overwhelmed by the experience and the thought of God's great act of condescension to his people, Zechariah must have stood rooted to the spot for a few more minutes while the astonishing ideas and images whirled about in his brain. When at last he could focus his attention again the angel was gone, and Zechariah gathered up the edge of his robe and backed toward the entryway.

Outside, the people had become fearful for the old priest's life. It was always an uneasy moment when a mortal approached the immediate Presence of God, and any delay in his return seemed ominous. It must have been a great relief for them to see him finally emerge, but when he could not speak to them to recite the great benediction which was his right to do, and when he excitedly tried to inform them with various gestures and expressions about the angel he had seen, they finally realized he had seen some sort of vision in the temple.

So Zechariah retired to his home in the hill country of Judea after his service was concluded, where he and his wife had plenty of time to contemplate what the Lord was about to do in their day.

I imagine that Zechariah and Elizabeth went back to the

Scriptures to see what they could learn about this unique child they were about to bear, and his relationship to the promised Messiah. There would have been many passages to examine, among them the magnificent words of Isaiah,

> A voice cries: "In the wilderness prepare the way of the LORD, make straight in the desert a highway for our God. Every valley shall be lifted up, and every mountain and hill be made low. . . . And the glory of the LORD shall be revealed, and all flesh shall see it together" (Isaiah 40:3-4a, 5a).

But of special interest would have been the words of Malachi which the angel had quoted. Malachi had been a man of great spiritual force whose love for the people of God was intense, even as his concept of God's expectations for His people was uncompromising. He knew that God's people had become lax in their duty and casual about their disobedience. He was absolutely convinced that God would come to bring deliverance to His people, but he knew as well that God would not overlook their sin. Yes, "the Lord whom you seek will suddenly come to his temple," he had written, "but who may abide the day of his coming? And who shall stand when he appears?

"For he is like a refiner's fire and like fuller's soap," Malachi had warned,

> He will sit as a refiner and purifier of silver, and he will purify the sons of Levi and refine them like gold and silver, till they present right offerings to the LORD. Then the offering of Judah and Jerusalem will be pleasing to the LORD as in the days of old and as in former years (Malachi 3:3-4).

In other words—as Zechariah could vouch on the basis of his brief encounter with the terrifying angel of the Lord—one might wish to think twice before rushing into the presence of the Lord unprepared. He himself had gone into the Holy Place only after careful washings, a ritual sacrifice, and the prayers of his fellow priests, and even then he had been overwhelmed with his own mortality when the angel of the Lord actually appeared to him.

God's people, Malachi knew, thought they were looking forward to His coming, but the question he raised for them was whether they were truly prepared for His holy presence. Zechariah, upon reflection, thought not. All the impurities which had become embedded in their souls would have to be removed before they could stand before the Lord.

And as he knew, this would not be a pleasant process. Malachi had likened it to refining gold and silver in the intense heat of a refiner's fire to remove the dross, or like the strong alkali soap the fuller used to bleach and whiten cloth. Until his people had been purified, Zechariah knew, they could not bear the scrutiny of their Maker.

But how could they be prepared? That was to be the job of his son, "to make ready a people prepared for the Lord." Zechariah could not have known how the Messiah himself would ultimately bear the heat of the refiner's fire, although the prophet Isaiah had said the Lord's servant would be "wounded for our transgressions" and "bruised for our iniquities." John's job, however, would be to persuade them to come to Him in the right spirit—a spirit of willingness to hear God's truth and embrace it with their whole heart.

We, too, are about to encounter the man who would claim to be the Lord's Messiah. But if we are to be able to see Him for who He truly is, we must come with the same openness of heart and spirit.

The Person God Chooses

(Luke 1:26-38)

If you were to travel north in Palestine from the Judean hills through Samaria, you would come at last to a great, sunken valley—a rift caused by a massive geological subsidence—separating the mountains of Galilee to the north from the central highlands to the south. Known in the Old Testament as the valley of Jezreel, this broad, rich plain, bordered on both sides by great limestone escarpments which mark the fault lines, was the site of numerous major battles throughout history. Here the good general Barak defeated Sisera during the time of the Judges. Gideon also, with his small band of trumpeters and torch-bearers ringing the edge of the valley by night, threw the Amalekites into confusion. King Saul's final battle against the Philistines took place here, ending tragically with his death, along with his sons, on Mount Gilboa on the southern edge of the valley. And here too, in the last days, John envisioned the final battle between the forces of good and evil at Armageddon.

Near the north rim, where the mountains of Lower Galilee are cleft by a small valley, you would come to the city of Nazareth, which was a tiny, insignificant village in Jesus' day. Nestled there within a circle of hills, Nazareth lay near the action, largely overlooked by the world and by history. Passing a few miles to the south through that great valley, the highway known as the "Way of the Sea" linked northern cities with the Mediterranean coast

23

and, ultimately, with Egypt. Great caravans and armies had traversed this route for centuries.

But Nazareth itself was content to focus on local matters: harvesting fruit, pasturing sheep and goats, and providing services to keep the economy solvent. It would have been a pretty little town, if poor; its small, flat-roofed houses surrounded by gnarled, wide-spreading fig trees, graceful, feathery palms, scented oranges, silvery olive trees, and thick hedges. Most of its people, while well aware of the armies and political movements which swept past their doorstep from time to time, would have been preoccupied with the local business of survival, of family, and of making a living.

Among those simple farmers and shepherds who called Nazareth their home nearly 2,000 years ago was a certain humble craftsman, a carpenter named Joseph, who supplied the people with simple furniture and the tools of their respective trades. Matthew gives a brief but significant picture of Joseph as a just and compassionate man who was willing to do whatever the Lord asked. If he was like his contemporaries among the working class in Galilee, he would not have considered marriage until he was in his mid- to late twenties.

By contrast, it was customary for girls to marry in their early teens. Thus it was likely that Joseph was nearing thirty when he became engaged to a young girl of perhaps fourteen or fifteen named Mary. Mary's background is unknown to us, but in a small town like Nazareth, the two would have been acquainted and both likely came from working-class families. Though poor, both could claim a distinguished heritage, tracing their ancestry all the way back to David, Israel's greatest king.

It is entirely possible that Joseph and Mary had met on their own, perhaps at a harvest festival, or at the single well which supplied the city then and is still in existence today—appropriately called Mary's Well. It would have been up to their parents to arrange the marriage, however, and when all parties had agreed, the engagement would have been formalized by a simple ceremony in which both sets of parents uttered a benediction, God's blessing, over them as they tasted a cup of wine together.

But as simple as the ceremony would have been, it was absolutely binding. Legally they were treated as a married couple from that moment forward. Had Joseph died, Mary would have been considered a widow. The agreement, in fact, could only be broken by an official divorce. Nevertheless, the couple would not live together until after the wedding, and it would have been unthinkable for Mary to risk her virginity before that day. The time between the engagement and their wedding would have been spent making all the necessary preparations relative to household, family, living arrangements, and so on.

As quaint and inviting as this humble setting may appear to us today, one should understand how it would have appeared to the religious establishment of that day. From the perspective of the highly educated and sophisticated people in Jerusalem and Judea, Galilee and the Galileans were objects of scorn and derision. Philosophically committed to learning and study as the highest good, the rabbis and the religious leaders would have regarded unlettered country folk like Joseph and Mary with utter contempt. It was inconceivable to them that anything good could come out of Nazareth.

But on one particular day in Nazareth, probably in mid-March of 5 B.C., the daily routine for the young woman Mary was about to be interrupted in a most astonishing way. Mary's family would have arisen early, as all Middle Eastern families do, in order to get as many of their tasks done as possible before the heat of the day. The morning air would have been crisp and cool, as the rainy season had just ended, and the hills around Nazareth would have been a rich green, in anticipation of a good harvest.

One of Mary's tasks would likely have been to go early to the village well, where she would fill a large earthenware jug with water, returning with it either on her shoulder or hip, even as young girls do to this day. Breakfast was usually a cake of bread, perhaps with olives or cheese inside, and a little dried fruit. We don't know what Mary's father did for a living, but the men and older boys in the family would have left early for the fields or the shop where they worked their craft or trade. The youngest child in the family would probably be assigned to tend the animals while the others went about their daily routine.

We are not told of anyone else witnessing Mary's remarkable visitor that morning, so perhaps her mother had gone to the local market to purchase the day's provisions—a routine activity where few means of preserving food are available. Mary may have stoked the fire and gotten out the handmill to begin grinding grain into flour for the day's supply of bread. We can picture her pouring grain through the hole in the center of the upper millstone and working the handle in a circular fashion while the crushed grain spilled out from between the two disc-shaped stones onto a cloth as fine flour, ready to be used for the day's baking.

Whatever she was doing, Mary was suddenly startled by a voice which greeted her with the words, "Hail, you who are highly favored! The Lord is with you." Now, that opening word translated "hail" in the Revised Standard Version or "greetings" in the New International Version, is really a much richer word. It carries with it something of the spirit of the Hebrew "shalom," meaning "peace" or "well-being." The Greek word communicates a deep, almost uncontainable joy. It was indeed a grand greeting for this young woman.

In a culture where men did not approach women directly, and where women stayed out of sight when visitors were present, the very fact that this man was speaking to her would have been a surprise in itself. But as she lifted her dark eyes to meet those of the speaker, she must have seen that this was no ordinary man. She could not yet have known that it was the angel Gabriel who had appeared to her kinsman, Zechariah, six months earlier in the temple in Jerusalem. From that lavish and holy temple in cosmopolitan Jerusalem, where we might have expected an angel to appear, God's primary messenger had come this day to a rude and humble peasant's quarters in the tiny, backwater community of Nazareth.

Yet it was not so much the presence of the angel himself which troubled this unpretentious young girl; what really troubled her, our text tells us, was what he said to her. "She was greatly troubled at his words, and considered in her mind what sort of greeting this might be." She, after all, was a nobody—a girl, from an obscure peasant family, in a little out-of-the-way community. Why would this impressive stranger suddenly be standing there telling her she was highly favored of God? "Me? Mary?" From what we know about her and about the straightforwardness and naivete of her faith, she must have been considering not only her humble social status but her own heart—and she did not feel she deserved such a greeting.

Knowing the likely effect of his troubling appearance and abrupt greeting, the angel encourages Mary not to be afraid, but repeats his astonishing message that God has taken special note of this young woman and desires to make her the object of His special favor. I am reminded of the words of God repeated by Isaiah in the forty-third chapter of his book, "Because you are precious in my eyes, and honored, and I love you"—you have found special favor with God. "He loves you!" the angel was saying. What an overwhelming message! Here she is—a simple young girl, going about her daily routine while trying to do simply what is expected of her, no doubt recognizing the weaknesses of her own character and assuming she will spend her days in an appropriate obscurity—and God says to her in effect, "You are precious in my eyes, Mary, and honored, and I love you." Then comes the most incredible part of the angel's announcement.

> Behold, you will conceive in your womb and bear a son, and you shall call his name Jesus. He will be great, and will be called the Son of the Most High; and the Lord God will give him the throne of his father David, and he will reign over the house of Jacob for ever; and of his kingdom there will be no end (Luke 1:31-33).

Can you imagine how astonishing such a message would be to this humble peasant girl?

Yet Mary does not seem particularly astonished, not nearly as astonished as we would be. She would have known what it was all about. The national religion may have lost its soul, but there were many in Israel who firmly anticipated the fulfillment of prophecy in the coming of a Messiah-Deliverer. Despite their humble circumstances, Mary would have been quite aware of her own heritage as one of the house and lineage of David. Interestingly, she does not protest, she does not question the theology of what is going on, but simply raises the most obvious question that a young girl just out of puberty might raise. "How shall this be, since I have no husband?"

The angel is equally straightforward in describing the miracle that is about to transpire. "The Holy Spirit will come upon you, and the power of the Most High will overshadow you; therefore the child to be born will be called holy, the Son of God."

Why is it that this miracle is so difficult for many of us to believe? That the Lord God who formed mankind from the dust of the earth and breathed into his nostrils the breath of life could impregnate one of his creation to form a human person in which His Spirit would reside does not seem at all unreasonable to me. What would be far more difficult to believe would be that any ordinary man, conceived and born as we all are in sin, could possibly be divine in any sense. A virgin birth seems a most appropriate and creative way for God to enter His world.

Mary was unlikely to have understood just how such a remarkable thing could take place, but her only question, a very practical one at that, had been answered and she was content to leave the matter in the hands of God. "Behold," she said simply, "I am the handmaid of the Lord; let it be to me according to your word." Mary had not learned to pray as we so often do, "Thy will be changed." She prayed, "Thy will be done," and the angel left her.

Mary's response seems so sweet and simple. "I am the hand-maid of the Lord; let it be to me according to your word." Don't think for a moment that she failed to understand the implications of this divine pregnancy. Living as we do in an age of promiscuity, we cannot begin to understand the personal and social devastation which would have accompanied a pregnancy out of wedlock in Mary's close-knit and moral society. Regardless of how it was handled, she was almost certain to lose her fiancé and perhaps the chance of ever being married, which would be devastating for a young woman in that culture. She would become something of a pariah to her own family, who were not likely to believe such a wild tale. In fact, had anyone wanted to make an example of her, the death penalty was still in effect for adultery.

As the poet Luci Shaw says,

> It seemed too much to ask
> of one small virgin
> that she should stake shame
> against the will of God . . .
> and it seems much
> too much to ask you, or me,
> to be part of the
> different thing—
> God's shocking, unorthodox,
> unheard of Thing,
> to further heaven's hopes
> and summon God's glory.[1]

Yes, I suppose for us it does seem too much to ask, for us who have risked so little for God, for us who have so little experience trusting him. But apparently for Mary it was different. She knew the risks were great. She had to know. Her easy acceptance could only have come from a trust that God knew what He was doing even if she did not; she trusted that God knew what He was doing even when He asked the hard thing of her. It comes from a soul which has learned to be content with whatever God says or does. It comes from a personal conviction that God's reward for obedience so totally overshadows its cost or inconvenience as to be unworthy of consideration.

All this Mary had to know, for all her youth and outward humble circumstances. She was in the habit of saying "Yes" to God, so He knew that despite all the world's contrary evaluations, He had found in this young girl the ideal person to bear His Son.

I wonder how many of us are really willing to do the hard thing today? I wonder how many of us even see a pure heart as desirable when our culture scorns it? I wonder how many of us make it our highest priority to cultivate such a pure heart through our honesty and simple obedience, taking the Lord at His word, willing to do the hard thing for the Lord's glory?

God weighs our hearts today exactly as he weighed hearts in Mary's day. It may be that he has as few to choose from now as he had then. We would do well to recall the blessing Jesus promised to people like His mother. "Blessed are those who are pure in heart," he said, "for they shall see God."

Note

1. Luci Shaw, "YES to Shame and Glory," *Christianity Today*, vol. 30, no. 18 (December 12, 1986): 22-24.

The Christmas Spirit

Stepping out of my office in Pennsylvania one sunny day several years ago, leaving the stained glass windows and beautiful antique furniture behind, I drove a few blocks to the heart of a ghetto area to which I had been summoned by an emergency call. Parking in the back alley (as I had been instructed by a neighbor to do in order to draw as little attention to my visit as possible), I picked my way to the door through broken glass and litter, shuddering to think that people actually lived under these circumstances. But my culture shock had only begun.

Pushing open the sagging door when no one responded to my polite knocking, I was overwhelmed by the stench and the squalor. Inside, as my informant had feared, I found a comatose elderly woman on the couch where she had lain for several days without food or water or attention. A plate containing some now unrecognizable provisions left by a neighbor lay at her side, and several mangy pets which had been shut in with her for several days eyed me suspiciously. Periodically, a shallow breath rasped through her parched throat, sounding to me like a threatening hiss from the death spirits which haunted this pit.

But the culture shock which jarred my senses that day as I passed from my pleasant, happy world into a place of decay and death must have been mild compared to the stunning contrast undergone by the Son of God as He left His heavenly realm to enter a world so contaminated and distorted by sin and death. This is all we have ever known and it is difficult, therefore, to appreciate the incarnation, to appreciate what an incredible step downward it was for God to take upon Himself the form of a man and to come and be born in our world. It is not too much to say that asking Jesus to take up residence on this planet would have been for Him far more repugnant than asking me to move into the tiny ghetto flat I just described. We need to understand what a remarkable thing God did for us in coming to this earth.

What from God's perspective was "the fulness of time" must not have seemed particularly timely to that obscure carpenter and his teenaged bride as they arrived in Bethlehem toward evening, after traveling some ninety miles over the course of four or five days—he on foot and she on the back of a donkey.

Augustus, the Roman emperor, had planned a census to set the stage for new taxes (politicians were about the same then as they are now), and King Herod, always anxious to please, must have laid the groundwork by issuing the orders for citizens of Palestine to be enrolled in their ancestral home. So Joseph, a direct descendant of David, was required to travel from his home in Nazareth to Bethlehem to be registered at the home of his forefathers. As Mary's child was due (and due early in relationship to their marriage), and as this would have been a scandal in their hometown of Nazareth, the young mother-to-be accompanied her new husband on this arduous journey.

And it was indeed an arduous journey—not at all a good time to travel. Perhaps they had been delayed from coming earlier by Mary's visit with Elizabeth. In any case by December, which it quite likely was, the rainy season had begun in earnest and temperatures had fallen. Many of the dirt trails which served as roads would quickly have become almost impassable in those heavy winter rains.

The most direct route to Bethlehem from Nazareth led southward through Samaria and the rugged hill country of Judea, but because of the Jews' discomfort with travel in Samaria and because of the treacherous nature of the terrain and the climate, it is likely that the young couple passed eastward along the Valley of Jezreel, which divided Judea and Galilee. From Beth-shan their route would have taken them into the great Rift Valley, through which the Jordan River flows southward from the Sea of Galilee down to the Dead Sea. Crossing over to the eastern side of the river, they would have found warmer temperatures and heavy rains a great deal less likely as they headed south toward the fords of Jericho, where their ancestors had crossed into the Promised Land so long ago. There they, too, could cross over the river once again back to Jerusalem and then head south a few miles to Bethlehem.

Though less hazardous, this route was longer than the more direct one through Samaria, and it would have taken them four or five days of steady travel to cover the ninety miles or more. Their donkey would have been carrying the few provisions this humble family required for living during their extended adventure. Many months were to pass before they were able to return to Nazareth.

The final leg of their journey could well have been the worst. Coming from as far away as Jericho that morning, or even the little inn along the way which Jesus made famous in His parable of the Good Samaritan, Mary and Joseph would have had to climb some 3,000 feet along a tortuous, winding route through the Judean desert before skirting the great city of Jerusalem and heading south through the Jerusalem hills toward their final destination.

We think travel is difficult today—we can only imagine how weary they must have felt and how great must have been their relief as the humble village of Bethlehem finally appeared above them, stretched along the upper slopes of the two hills where it had lain since long before the birth of their ancestor David. In fact, as the shortened winter day darkened around them, they would have climbed through the very fields and terraced gardens which had also welcomed Ruth from across the Jordan to this place where she had become the wife of Boaz and given birth to her first-born son, Obed. He in turn had become the father of Jesse, who was the father of David, the greatest king Israel ever knew.

Mary and Joseph knew that their special child was going to be born in Bethlehem, this child whom the angel had said would occupy the throne of his father David. I am sure they could not have understood it, and I am sure at that weary moment they must have wondered greatly what God had in mind. But they must also have experienced considerable relief as they approached their destination after such an exhausting journey, Mary probably already feeling the contractions of early labor.

As they passed the Migdal Eder, "the tower of the flock" from which Rabbinic writings said the Messiah would be revealed, I imagine they were too tired to pay much attention to the shepherds there keeping watch over their flocks, flocks destined for sacrifice at the temple in Jerusalem. Nor could those shepherds have known that this apparently insignificant couple trudging past in the waning light carried with them the greatest gift the world would ever know—the sacrifice which would end forever the sacrifices from which they gained their living at the temple.

In town, their worst fears were realized. Weary from their travels and not a little anxious about Mary's labor, they came at last to the inn, or kahn, in which travelers stayed—only to find it had long since been filled to overflowing with merchants from the caravans. Along with other travelers, they had bedded down for the night within the walled enclosure which gave them a measure of safety from the hazards they had faced along the roads.

Where could they go if the kahn were filled and so many others from the tribe of David had filled every available room in Bethlehem? Mary's contractions were likely becoming more and more persistent now, and they had to wonder whether this strange adventure would end alongside the road with the unprotected birth of their miracle child. I expect the young carpenter must have begun to feel desperate about his inability to care for his vulnerable young family.

Many of our Christmas stories present the innkeeper in a bad light, but I think we should not fault the one who finally did provide them some hospitality. He could hardly have put his other guests out in the street. I imagine him standing in the lighted doorway, peering over Joseph's shoulder at the young woman, perhaps huddled beside the donkey to absorb another contraction. He may have felt compassion, and perhaps the desperation, himself. How could he help this couple? He simply couldn't turn them away. Taking a lamp from beside the stand by the door and pulling his robe around him for warmth, he likely stepped out into the darkness, beckoning the young couple to follow him.

At the back of the kahn was a small cave—one of many which perforated the limestone cliffs in the hills surrounding Bethlehem. The enclosure would likely have been built up against those cliffs, and the cave would have been used to shelter animals from the brisk winter nights and the rain. "Nothing fancy," the innkeeper probably explained as he led them inside, "but we'll put out some clean straw and it will be warm and sheltered. By tomorrow we should be able to find you some place more suitable." I expect Mary even appreciated the measure of privacy the little stable would provide on this momentous evening.

Sometime during the night, perhaps while Joseph busied himself collecting water or tearing strips of cloth from an extra garment in which to wrap the child (it would not have been proper for him to be present during the actual delivery), Mary gave birth to her first-born son, as the angel had predicted. It may be that little Mary, fourteen or fifteen years old, had to deliver the child herself, since the Bible makes no mention of any other visitors, and such things did happen from time to time in those days; or it may be that Joseph called upon some older woman among the travelers for help. But however it was, the Son of God entered the world that night on the floor of a simple stable, where He was subsequently wrapped in strips of cloth and laid on fresh straw, probably in a manger chipped out of the limestone walls of a cave.

In the quietness of the night, before the shepherds arrived, I can imagine the two young parents holding each other and gazing in awe at this tiny child and wondering out loud what in the world God must have in mind! So many unusual circumstances had already surrounded His birth.

Had they known more, perhaps they would have understood less. Even their extreme circumstances didn't give them categories to understand how truly extraordinary the event was. This child had not simply come from Mary's womb. He had actually come from heaven to be born under these rude conditions. The contrast between His home in heaven and this place where He had come to be in our midst must have been greater than anything they could imagine.

I don't think we quite understand the significance of Christmas. We think of home and family and pleasant surroundings. We think of indulging ourselves. But on that first Christmas, Jesus Christ was certainly not indulging himself. He had become poor so that we could become rich. That is really what the incarnation means: He set aside all the glorious riches of heaven to be born in a crude stable. He stepped out of a world of perfection and splendor to take up residence in a place of distortion and death. He gave up His place at God's right hand to wander from city to city, residing periodically in borrowed accommodations. He gave up a position in which all His needs were certainly fulfilled to experience hunger and thirst and exhaustion and disappointment and grief and betrayal and fear and pain. Although through Him God had breathed life into the universe, He would experience, ultimately, what it meant to die. He did not have to do that, but He chose to do so because He loved us.

It is an incomprehensible irony that the One who could command legions of angels would let Himself be led away by a small band of uncertain commandos under an alien authority. The One who had helped hurl the stars into place would let simple men drive spikes through the very hands which had formed them. The One who enjoyed the freedom of unencumbered purity would take upon Himself the pollution of a world of sinners. Do you understand the awesome nature of the incarnation?

But that, of course, is what Christmas is all about. It is about the incarnation. It is about the birth of a man "Who," as the apostle Paul told us, "being in very nature God, did not count equality with God something to be grasped." He did not consider that He had to hold onto His status, to His privileged position; rather, He "made himself nothing, taking the very nature of a servant, being made in human likeness. And being found in appearance as a man, he humbled himself and became obedient to death, even death on a cross!"

We talk a lot about "the Christmas spirit," but what is it? It cannot simply be sentiment and good cheer. The Christmas spirit has to be the spirit of the One in whose honor we celebrate this grand holiday. That is what Paul says to us in Philippians: "Your attitude should be the same as that of Christ Jesus" (Philippians 2:5, NIV). Do you want to know about the Christmas spirit? Then look at Christ. I somehow doubt there is much of this spirit reflected in our frantic buying or even in our giving—the bulk of which is to people who don't need very much.

By contrast, the Christmas spirit, the spirit of Christ, is a radical spirit of self-giving to people whose needs are profound—even when the gift is unacknowledged or even spurned. The Christmas spirit is giving anyway out of a spirit of compassion and love. Philippians 2:1-2 (NIV) sums up the true Christmas spirit that will be reflected in those who have received it from Christ: "If you have any encouragement from being united with Christ, if any comfort from his love, if any fellowship with the Spirit, if any tenderness and compassion," then you should be "like-minded," loving others in the same way. That is the Christmas spirit.

I wonder—how many of us have actually come to Christmas with a commitment to reach out in a tangible way to someone beyond the circle of those we already love and who already love us? Can we, like Jesus, set aside our own convenience, and give ourselves to those whom we perceive to be unlovely? Here alone we will find the joy for which our spirits long. For that is the spirit of Christ, and of Christmas.

Shepherds, Why This Jubilee?

The stars are brilliant, unimaginably so, in a desert sky at night. I have seen them hanging at intervals in a three-dimensional sky, crowded against a vast backdrop of light from a million billion individual suns. I have always thought that people who speak of the "dark void of outer space" were revealing more of an inner void, a lack of imagination, a certain blindness to reality, for the universe is not empty. Vast, yes, it is incomprehensibly vast, but it is not empty! There is simply room in it—room for a thousand worlds like our own, room for an eternity of exploration, room for dimensions beyond those our eyes can normally see, room for the things of the spirit—room, perhaps, even for angels.

The shepherds who had bedded their charges down in the marah, or sheep fold, close under a bluff in fields perhaps a mile or two from Bethlehem that momentous night, were quite familiar with such a sky. All their lives they had drawn light and life from these distant and mysterious sources—warmth and energy and resplendent light from the solar furnace which burned its way across the sky by day, and a cool, enchanting luminosity from the moon and stars which transformed the familiar landscape at night. Unlike the world which future generations would find shrouded in the haze of civilization, they were used to looking into the soul of the universe.

But I think that night they were unprepared for what they would see. At sundown they had urged their unruly little flocks into the marah, calling out the familiar names, their faithful dogs blustering about, adding exclamation points to their commands. When the activity had died away and the sheep were safe for the night, these simple men, heirs to an occupation practiced already for nearly two millennia among these hills, would have kindled a fire near the gate and sat down to draw their crude meal from the leather scrips hanging from their shoulders.

As the evening wore on and the chill night air crept around them, they would have drawn their lambskin mantles close as they sat and talked or rested by the shifting light of the fire. If you had been there, you would have seen a circle of rough-looking men with coarse hair, rugged complexions, and matted beards. But the rough, almost savage exterior masked hearts made tender by years of caring for things lovable and helpless. They were simple-minded men whose lives were completely preoccupied by the few, primitive responsibilities they held in common. Their conversation would certainly have been about the sheep, and perhaps the weather, and remembrances of moments of courage and surprise. If their topics seem dull and trivial to us, we should recall that the movement of kingdoms and armies, the latest styles and practices, even shifting theories of life and the movements of the universe were all alike irrelevant to them. This was their universe, and it mattered most that they knew what to expect from it and how to shape it to their advantage.

More than that, these shepherds knew their God. They had not been distracted from God by a thousand things, as we are. It is likely that the sheep they tended were the very ones used for the sacrifices at the temple in Jerusalem, for we know that the temple flocks were kept in the vicinity of Bethlehem. Perhaps they reflected from time to time on the costliness of sin which took the lives of the sheep they were commissioned to nurture. And no doubt they spoke on occasion about the risks involved in their own role as the sheep's defenders. Good as they were with their slings, the sudden assault of a marauding lion, bursting upon them in the darkness, had taken the life of more than one faithful shepherd. Jesus was later to say, "The Good Shepherd lays down his life for his sheep." It was indeed a high-risk occupation.

Living that close to the reality of death was incentive enough for them to go up to the synagogue from time to time to purify themselves, to be sure they were at peace with their Maker. There they would listen with childlike faith to the very words of God as they were read to them from the Torah. As the author Lew Wallace says in his *Tale of the Christ:*

> In a verse of the Shema they found all the learning and all the law of their simple lives—that their Lord was One God, and that they must love him with all their souls. And they loved him, and such was their wisdom, surpassing that of kings.[3]

In that security the shepherds drifted off, one by one, to a dreamless and satisfying sleep there on the uneven ground before the fire. Only the one designated as watchman stayed awake, pacing back and forth by the gate, listening, perhaps, to the distant cry of a jackal followed by a slight stirring among the sheep, waiting until the profound stillness of the desert embraced him once again.

He had heard (or rather *felt*) that silence many times before. But this time it was different. This seemed to be the silence of expectancy, as if all nature were holding its breath and every ear were turned upward in anticipation, waiting for a word—The Word—for which all creation had waited since the dawn of time. A chill ran through his body. He had the uncanny feeling he was not alone. Though he was no coward, he shuddered at the thought of an unseen enemy stalking him in the darkness. Instinctively backing toward the fire and the company of his friends, he suddenly cried out in terror, for there before him, in a place occupied by nothing more threatening than a rocky outcropping only a moment earlier, stood a man—but such a man!

Awakened by the cry, the other shepherds leapt to their feet, staffs in hand, feeling their scrips for sling stones, ready to meet the enemy. But what they saw instantly froze them in fear. Any ordinary enemy they could face with confidence, but the terror awakened in them by the sight of this man was preternatural. This man was surrounded by an otherworldly brilliance which seared and dazzled them. They knew instinctively that all their weapons would be useless. The terror they felt was not the ominous threat of a great Evil, but the terrifying exposure of their own souls before a great and awesome Good.

These shepherds were not the first to feel the terror of standing in the presence of the glory of the Lord. Abraham, Moses, and Isaiah before them had experienced such a dread encounter. The shepherds may have felt they shared a common experience with these great men as they stood before the devouring fire in that awesome place.

It is not coincidental that Luke tells us the shepherds were filled with fear as the glory of the Lord shone around them. Anyone in his right mind would have been. The glory of the Lord illuminated their own sinful and polluted souls, and they were stricken with terror. As C. S. Lewis observed about the great lion, Aslan, it is not "safe" in the presence of God. We are not prepared to respond to that good news if we have not first of all trembled in the presence of the Living God as the shepherds did! "The fear of the Lord is the beginning of wisdom," quotes Solomon in one of the Proverbs. If you and I do not fear God, we shall never appreciate the good news of the gospel which the angels brought that night.

If it was a compelling fear which had prepared the shepherds to respond to the gospel, that fear was quickly replaced by a compelling interest. "Be not afraid," the angel had said—I don't want you to fear because I have a special message for you which supersedes your fear. "I bring you good news of a great joy which will come to all the people; for to you is born this day in the city of David a Savior, who is Christ the Lord," the Messiah for whom you have been waiting for generations!

When the announcement was made that the words spoken by the prophets concerning the Messiah had come to pass, the shepherds' response indicates they were greatly moved and excited by this revelation. They knew what the coming of the Messiah could mean to them and to their people. That mysterious prediction which had haunted their hopes and dreams for so many generations was now being fulfilled! They had heard it from their fathers and their grandfathers and their great grandfathers before them; and now here it was, taking place before their very eyes.

There was no doubting the authority of the announcement. Their minds were filled with awe and wonder as they listened to the voice they imagined Daniel must have heard beside the river Ulai. This wondrous creature before them must be the angel Gabriel, God's special messenger, about whom they had heard often enough; but to see him standing before them was unimaginable.

"And this will be a sign for you," the angel continued, "you will find a babe wrapped in swaddling cloths and lying in a manger." It was a tacit invitation for them to come and experience the good news firsthand. If they wished to confirm this announcement for themselves, they were welcome to do so.

And then it was as if the dark air around the shepherds began to shimmer with light which became more substantial, suddenly erupting into life as a great company of the heavenly host appeared with the angel, voicing the unrestrained joy of creation in response to that announcement: "Glory to God in the highest, and on earth peace among men with whom he is pleased."

For a few glorious minutes, the heavens rang with the magnificent chorus of the angels. And then, as suddenly as they had come, the angels disappeared into heaven. Once again the night was still and dark, but this time the shepherds were not so certain it was empty. If only they had eyes to see, they felt they would find themselves still surrounded by the heavenly hosts, as Elisha and his servant did when they were under siege from the king of the Arameans. They had heard that story many times and remembered that Elisha had prayed concerning his servant's fears, "'O LORD, open his eyes so he may see.' [And] the LORD opened the servant's eyes, and he looked and saw the hills full of horses and chariots of fire all around Elisha" (2 Kings 6:17, NIV).

Perhaps it was like that now! Maybe they simply had not seen it before; but they were surrounded by the glory of God, and by His messengers. For a while no one spoke. I would not be surprised if at that moment no one was aware of anyone else in the world. But this was a critical moment. They had heard the good news. How would they respond?

You and I have been there, listening to the good news. But very quickly the world again intrudes. That brief moment of epiphany fades so suddenly and we find ourselves alone again with our familiar props and with the pressing responsibilities for the sheep. When the moment has passed, we wonder—could it have been real? Could God actually have reached down and touched the earth . . . *our* earth? Could He have spoken to us?

I imagine the shepherds looked at one another as if to say, "Will you tell me you saw it, too?" And then the hillside erupted with enthusiasm as the shepherds, too transparently honest to convince each other of a more believable lie, began to grip each other by the shoulders, eagerness lighting their rough faces, and to say, Let's go! "Let us go over to Bethlehem and see this thing that has happened, which the Lord has made known to us."

So they did. The shepherds would not be content until they had seen the truth with their own eyes and touched it with their own hands, until they had offered the true worship of their own hearts, until they had expressed their acceptance of the salvation offered by the Lord.

So "they went with haste, and found Mary and Joseph, and the babe lying in the manger." While what they saw probably did very much resemble what we imagine in our nativity scenes, nevertheless it would have been quite unimpressive to unbelieving eyes. There was nothing to distinguish the scene from a thousand other births to simple rural folk. No halo hung round the infant's head to make His identity unmistakable. The wise men were still several days away and the cattle had not gathered around the manger, compelled by some sixth sense to rivet their attention on the child who had usurped their feeding trough. Even the angels were gone. There was only the stable, the familiar smell of animals and straw; and to one side, barely illumined by perhaps nothing more than a small lamp, were the two young parents, transfixed by their first-born son.

But the shepherds saw so much more than that because they were looking at the scene through the eyes of believers. They had heard and believed the announcement by the angel, and therefore they were moved to worship and awe by the simple evidence of God's love which lay before them. A compelling interest had drawn them to set aside every other priority (did you stop to think what was happening to the sheep while they were gone?) and to say, "This is what it is all about! For this I would give up my life itself. This is where God has touched the earth."

The next step, of course, was quite natural and spontaneous. "When they saw it, they made known the saying which had been told them concerning this child." I expect on their way through the crowded courtyard that night, where the rest of the guests were camped—merchants from a passing caravan and many pilgrims there for the census—the shepherds likely awakened many weary travelers. As they left the little cave at the back of the enclosure, they amazed the skeptical travelers with animated accounts of the visitation by the angels and the precise prediction of what they would find in the cave. Evidently they told the story with such enthusiasm and conviction that, "all who heard it wondered at what the shepherds told them." The shepherds' firsthand experience of the gospel gave them a compelling witness. They had found the word to be true. They did not have to complete an eleven-week course on evangelism. Like John, they simply told what they had seen and heard.

> That which we have seen and heard declare we unto you, that ye [you] also may have fellowship with us: and truly our fellowship is with the Father, and with his Son Jesus Christ (1 John 1:3, KJV).

They had heard a believable account of the coming of the Christ, they had witnessed the reality of this event themselves, and their conviction gave power to their testimony.

In the end, the shepherds returned to their work with the flocks, but things would never be the same for them. Luke says they returned, "glorifying and praising God for all they had heard and seen, as it had been told them." The climactic phase of their response to the gospel was compelling praise. No one who has truly encountered Christ can ever be the same again. These rough shepherds, who were often excluded from formal worship because their work made it difficult for them to remain ritually clean, returned to their work overflowing with spontaneous joy and praise.

In the great eighteenth-century French Christmas carol, "Angels We Have Heard on High," the onlookers ask, "Shepherds, why this jubilee? Why your joyous strains prolong? What the gladsome tidings be which inspire your heavenly song?" Their spirit of joy and gladness at their discovery is contagious. And when asked the reason for their celebration, they reply, "Come to Bethlehem and see Him whose birth the angels sing; come, adore on bended knee Christ the Lord, the newborn King."

I wonder if our joy is so contagious. If we truly understand who it was in the manger that night, if we are convinced the Maker of the universe stepped down from His throne to walk among us. I should think our witness would be every bit as compelling. Perhaps we may learn to be as bold and transparent as the shepherds, without even a thought of apology inviting to the manger those who inquire about our celebration.

Note

1. Lew Wallace, *Ben Hur: A Tale of the Christ* (New York: Harper & Brothers, 1880), 56.

The Peace That Passes Understanding

Mary and Joseph had just been given an awesome and almost impossible task—to raise a deliverer for their people. Nevertheless, they accepted the job and did their best with God's help. All they could do was trust Him for the results. At times their faith faltered and they became anxious about the boy, as Mary admits in Luke 2:48. But their job was to be obedient; God alone could manage the outcome.

With the circumcision of their son, Joseph and Mary acknowledged the fundamental truth that ultimately the care and nurture of a child demanded far more than they could possibly give. They wanted to claim God's covenant promises for their son.

It was at this ceremony that every Jewish boy received his name. Names were tremendously important to the Jews, as perhaps they should be to us. They believed that a name expressed something intrinsic about the person. In this case they could be especially assured because the angel Gabriel had specifically instructed both Joseph and Mary on separate occasions that the child's name was to be Yeshua, or Joshua—the name of Moses' successor who had led the children of Israel out of the wilderness and into the Promised Land. Later generations would prefer the Greek form of the name, Jesus, but in any language the name means "God saves" or "God is salvation." I am sure the parents of Jesus claimed that promise without comprehending the fullness of its application to their son.

Forty days after that special moment, a dramatic incident occurred which must have confirmed their faith in God's intention to care for them and for their child. They had packed up the things they needed for their two-hour journey to Jerusalem—Mary seated on the donkey once more, this time holding the bundled child in her arms—and had set out for the city of David, the center of the covenant life of Israel. Upon their arrival in Jerusalem they had come to the temple.

As usual, it was filled with busy people, the air heavy with the smells of incense and burning flesh from the sacrifices. The young couple with their six-week-old baby must have stepped hesitantly through the passageway known as "The Beautiful Gate" and looked across the courtyard toward the circular steps leading up to the "Court of Israel." Like their parents before them, and their grandparents, and all their ancestors for over a thousand years, they had come to the temple in accordance with the laws of Moses to offer the sin offering appropriate after the birth of a child. In addition, they would be consecrating their firstborn son to the Lord, an act which recalled the sparing of the firstborn of Israel on that night in Egypt when God's angel passed over the homes of His people but struck down the firstborn of the unrepentant Egyptians.

Mary and Joseph brought enough money for a pair of turtle-doves or two pigeons, as much as their poverty allowed. Their sacrifice was combined with others who came at the same time, and at the appropriate moment, they were summoned up onto the steps as the priest placed the offering on the altar and offered up prayers on their behalf, which seemed to ascend to heaven with the smoke from the altar of incense. Their ritual obligation complete, they descended the steps once again, but may well have waited, mingling with the crowd, in awe of the magnificent temple and the mysterious rituals which seemed somehow to bring them in touch with the God of their ancient fathers.

Suddenly, appearing out of the smoke and the crowd, an old man stepped up to them, his eyes shining. The startled parents looked on in amazement as this elderly gentleman gathered the baby Jesus into his wizened arms, looked toward heaven and, in deep gratitude, offered a remarkable prayer and prophecy.

While Mary and Joseph could not have known it at the time, this man, Simeon, was a devout and righteous man who had what was then the rare gift of the Holy Spirit. There is no indication that Simeon held any official position in the church. He was not a priest. He was a devout layman and God had touched him with His Spirit in a unique and powerful way. This same Spirit had revealed to him some time previously that he would not see death before he had seen the Messiah, promised for so long by the prophets of Israel—"the Lord's salvation." Like the watchman on the city wall, Simeon had waited anxiously for this day.

On this particular morning the Spirit had urged him to go to the temple and wait. We can only imagine the excitement which must have quickened his heart as he hurried through the busy streets, arriving at last at the holy place. What would he see? This grand conclusion to all the prophecies of Israel—what would he see in the Lord's Christ? Would some impressive royal figure be arriving at the temple? Or, maybe the opposite—maybe a revolutionary prophet out of the wilderness would be standing there, announcing God's judgment and the climax of history. He could only guess in what form the long-awaited Messiah would appear. He, too, must have stood there that day, peering through the haze and the crowd and the bustle, eyeing the worshipers as they hurried in and out, waiting for some unmistakable sign from the Spirit.

Then, at last, it came. "There, Simeon, there he is! The chosen One! There is the Messiah!" Simeon looked. A child? A mere infant? Why, the parents themselves were hardly more than children! Yet Simeon had walked with the Lord too long to doubt even the most unlikely answer to his prayers. So this was the One—the Messiah, the Light of the World, the Consolation of Israel. "Lord," he said, gathering that infant child into his arms and looking down into His face,

> now lettest thou thy servant depart in peace, according to thy word; for mine eyes have seen thy salvation which thou hast prepared in the presence of all peoples, a light for revelation to the Gentiles, and for glory to thy people Israel.

The song was beautiful, an utterly fitting carol to mark the birth of the Christ child. All the warmth and the joy and the peace which we strive to recreate every Christmas flowed smoothly and naturally from the old man's heart through his quivering lips as he claimed that promise. As his words trailed off, the unassuming little trio surrounding the baby must have felt like an island in a vast ocean of oblivious humanity.

But just as the astonished parents began to grasp some of the impact of his words, Simeon turned to them with eyes brimming with wisdom and compassion. "Behold," he said to Mary,

> this child is set for the fall and rising of many in Israel, and for a sign that is spoken against (and a sword will pierce through your own soul also), that thoughts out of many hearts may be revealed.

It was, if you will, the dark side of Christmas. Surely this lovely little dark-eyed baby had been born to humble parents, wrapped in swaddling clothes, and laid in a manger. Ruddy-cheeked shepherds had stood in amazement and wonder over this infant to whom the angel choirs had directed them. Even now, wise men from distant lands in the East searched the night skies for direction as they journeyed across mountain and desert to lay their lavish gifts at the feet of this peasant child.

But Christmas is not all sweetness and light. Our lives are still troubled by reality. Our loved ones still die, our relationships still disappoint us, our own conduct is still a source of discouragement to us. I think it is helpful to know that Christmas is also babies slain by a king in a jealous rage. It is a portent of a traitor in the dark. It is jeering soldiers and an angry mob shouting, screaming, "Crucify Him!" It is a tortured death, and bottomless grief, and despair, and fear. Christmas has no meaning without the crucifixion. The salvation Christ came to give us had to be purchased at a terrible price.

God had revealed to this devout man, Simeon, that His salvation had arrived in the person of an innocent-looking little baby. But Simeon was under no illusion that the grip of sin and death upon God's creation could be broken without a serious struggle. His eyes had indeed seen God's salvation, but they had also seen the sacrifice involved in accomplishing that salvation, as well as the frightening chasm which would divide those who accepted Christ's salvation from those who rejected it. The fall and rising of many would depend upon their response to this, the Lord's Christ.

It is unlikely Simeon knew exactly how God would deal with our sins and win our salvation. It is doubtful he could have discerned the shape of the coming kingdom of God. What he could see—and what is so important for you and for me as we look at Christmas and the reality of our own lives—is that God was still in control, that He had made certain promises, and that He intended to fulfill those promises for the care and the nurture of His children, whatever the cost.

It is here that we can find a great lesson in Simeon's song. Looking ahead, Simeon could see the road of life strewn with traps and pitfalls and various obstacles. He knew that Mary's heart would be grieved, that she would suffer a deep pain, that many others would as well. Yet Simeon's reaction is one of great peace. Death itself was a welcome guest—"Lord, now lettest thou thy servant depart in peace." He is talking about his death, not merely departing from the temple. How can that be?

I believe the answer lies in that first line; in fact, in the very first word, which is the Greek word *despota* ("Sovereign"). He uses this word to address God. It is one of the harshest words he could have chosen, one rarely used in the New Testament. From it we get our English word *despot*. Simeon would choose such a word only to refer to God's absolute control of life and of His world.

I know that scares some of us. We are not sure we want to have God controlling our lives. That is the source of much of our rebellion, because we want to maintain control for ourselves. We spend our lives resisting His control and His authority. But for Simeon, it was a source of great peace to know God was absolutely in control of His universe. Therefore His promises could not fail. And Simeon's peace should have been a source of encouragement to the two young parents who faced such a challenging future with their miracle child. Like Simeon, they could only be obedient and trust God to accomplish His purposes, whatever happened.

What is it, after all, that gives a child peace? Why is it that an infant whose existence is threatened at every moment can rest so securely in his mother's or father's arms? It is because the one who has accepted that responsibility gives security to the one cared for. All of us have experienced this sometime in our lives. It is what makes it possible for us as children to sleep in the back seat of the car.

As a child, returning late from some event, often in the wintertime, there were all sorts of treacherous things like icy roads that might face me and my family on our way home. Nevertheless, I recall sleeping soundly and peacefully in the back seat because my father was in charge, the controls were in his hands. He had committed himself to care for me and love and protect me along with the rest of my family, and I trusted him. Ultimately, our security rests in the fact that it is God who has undertaken our care and the controls are securely in His hands.

Many people today seem to fear God's sovereignty. They seem to fear God's complete control of the world and the universe. They want to take back the control of their lives, but with it they find that they have also accepted responsibility for things that are beyond their ability to control. If we refuse to acknowledge God's sovereignty over us, then we have to face all of those problems on our own. If we exclude Him from the management of our finances, then we have to walk the precarious tightrope over bankruptcy and recession and inflation and job security all by ourselves, with no assurance that anyone will be there to bail us out if we fail. If we choose to live the way we please, then we risk any and all possible consequences of our choices. If, on the other hand, we will live as God has called us to live, the results are in His hands. Ultimately, if we reject God's sovereignty, we must face death one-on-one, alone.

Simeon knew that such action was foolishness. Even supposing one could negotiate that treacherous path around fiscal and moral bankruptcy, what good would it do when he reached the other end and found it disappearing into the black void of death?

What Simeon had was a peace that passed all understanding. It was a peace which grew out of an ultimate trust in God. It was an example to the young parents of Jesus, as well as to all of us. It acknowledged the reality of evil and suffering which touch all of us and our children after us. But it found its ultimate confidence in the fact that God knows what He is doing, that He has made certain remarkable promises to us and to our children after us, and that if we will only commit ourselves to walk with Him, He will bring it to pass.

That is the promise Simeon claimed on that first Christmas, and you and I may claim it as well. The peace that passes all understanding, that supersedes any grief and lays to rest any anxiety, belongs to those alone who place their lives and their loved ones in the hands of a sovereign and compassionate God.

Wise Men Still Seek Him

(Matthew 2:1-12)

They were pagans, really, those wise men who, along with their improbable camels, found their way into Bethlehem that night, probably in February, 750 A.U.C. They were quite unaware they were stumbling into a thousand variations of the nativity scene. "A.U.C." stands for the Latin "in the year from the city's foundation," and designates the approximate date of the founding of Rome. Now, 750 years later, at the height of Rome's power, a caravan of Persian magi had arrived in an obscure rural village about five miles south of Jerusalem, led by certain astrological events they had witnessed across a thousand miles of desert to the temporary home of a peasant woman and her newborn son.

How could they have gotten there, these Zoroastrian priests, raised and educated on a dualistic philosophy of good and evil featuring the pagan god Ahura Mazda? Was it some wild coincidence that their interpretation of an apparently rare conjunction of planets and the appearance of an evanescent or fading star had led them to Bethlehem at the very moment of Christ's birth?

Scholars and astronomers agree that two years earlier these students of the stars would have observed a rare phenomenon in the heavens—a conjunction of the two brightest planets, Jupiter and Saturn, in the constellation Pisces. It was an event which takes place in the circulation of the planets only once every 805 years, and because of its brilliance and uniqueness would have caused quite a stir among those who interpreted life by the arrangement of the stars and the planets. Jupiter, the largest planet, was associated with gods and kings; and Saturn, with its rings, was considered to be the shield and defender of Palestine. The constellation Pisces, also associated with Palestine, represented epochal events and crises. The obvious conclusion, to an astrologer, was that some great king or god was about to appear in Palestine, perhaps bringing its history to some extraordinary climax.

Even more remarkable, the planet Mars joined that conjunction of planets the following year, creating a spectacular scene in the heavens. Interestingly, two 805-year cycles later, in the early seventeenth century, the great astronomer Johannes Kepler observed the same conjunction of planets and was amazed to discover that when the three planets were aligned, a new, extraordinarily brilliant and peculiarly colored evanescent star was visible between Jupiter and Saturn, something that he as an astronomer had never seen before. Whether the same phenomenon occurred just prior to Christ's birth or not, we cannot be certain, though it is a possibility. It is also interesting that the Chinese, who kept extremely accurate records, note the appearance of a comet in the same location at the very time the wise men would have been arriving in Jerusalem. And that comet would have been visible in the southern sky, from Jerusalem, looking directly toward Bethlehem. So all kinds of things were happening in the heavens at that particular moment in time.

Based on the reaction of Herod to kill all the boy babies born during the previous two years in Bethlehem, we can assume that the priest-sages had observed the unusual conjunction of planets two years earlier, had studied Jewish sources and learned of the promised Messiah, and had then headed for Palestine to witness this remarkable event firsthand and pay their homage to this new Messiah-King. Upon arriving in Jerusalem, their natural destination as it was the heart of the Jewish homeland, they were informed that the prophets had specifically listed Bethlehem as the birthplace of the Messiah.

Not surprisingly for them, as they set out from the city they now saw either the comet or perhaps some other manifestation of God's leading—even I suppose the shekinah glory, the bright light which had led the children of Israel in the wilderness. Whatever it was, as they pursued this opportunity to learn something of the God who had created the stars, (and who, obviously to them, controlled those stars and planets), they found themselves at last in the presence of an infant, only a few weeks old, but who had, in their eyes, received the divine imprint. There was no doubt in their minds that God had led them to this child, and they bowed down, as our text from Matthew tells us, and paid Him homage. They worshiped Him. They shared gifts of gold, frankincense and myrrh—gifts which symbolized His royalty, His humanity, and His divinity.

Now, why did God honor their search? The answer to that question is tremendously significant. I believe God honored the search precisely because these men truly desired to honor Him. The magi were not born in Palestine, they were not taught the Hebrew Scriptures, they had not witnessed God's miraculous deliverance of Israel; they had none of the advantages we have today in terms of access to the truth. But deep in their hearts they desired to know God, and they were willing to seize every available opportunity which might help them come to know His truth.

Paul's letter to the Romans confirms the culpability of those who claim not to have had an opportunity to know God. Paul says we all have the opportunity to know God. In Romans 1, beginning with verse 19, he says,

> What can be known about God is plain to them, because God has shown it to them. Ever since the creation of the world his invisible nature, namely, his eternal power and deity, has been clearly perceived in the things that have been made. So they are without excuse; for although they knew God they did not honor him as God or give thanks to him, but they became futile in their thinking and their senseless minds were darkened.

As we come to understand from the Scriptures how God works, we see that the wise men were rewarded in their search precisely because they were willing to honor God and give thanks to Him. Had they been unwilling to do that, their speculation about the nature of things would have become futile, God's Word predicts, and their minds would have been darkened to the truth. It was not that the astrology which guided their lives was the best source of information about the truth; rather, many people following that source have found their hearts darkened and their thinking futile. But these men honestly sought to know God and to honor Him as God.

Through the prophet Jeremiah in the Old Testament, God had promised that, "You will seek me and find me; when you seek me with all your heart." With a bit more explanation, another prophet, Isaiah, said, "Seek the LORD while he may be found, call upon him while he is near . . . let him return to the LORD, that he may have mercy on him, and to our God, for he will abundantly pardon" (Isaiah 55:6,7). It is a promise that those who come honestly seeking will surely find Him.

But what is the path by which we may find Him? The word translated "to seek" in Isaiah actually means "to tread." It is a challenge to take the specific steps necessary to find the Lord. The magi crossed a wilderness fraught with many dangers and risks to their own comfort and security in order to follow the pathway of truth to the Living God. You and I have been invited upon an adventure to seek God as well.

But seeking God, you understand, is more than just a mental exercise. As with the wise men, it involves the abandoning of the old life and a whole-hearted turning to the Lord, a willingness to respond to whatever leading He gives you, no matter how difficult or how risky. Those who want to play mind games with God and with truth will get nowhere. He makes Himself available to those alone who sincerely desire to know Him, intending to follow Him. Thus he concludes with the challenge not only to turn away from our own evil path, but ultimately to "return to the Lord"— not only to repent but to obey, to follow the Lord.

The path to knowing God, then, is two-fold—we must turn away from our pride and self-indulgence and sin, and turn to Him, with a commitment to follow Him as He uncovers His will for us. At whatever point we refuse to obey, we have stalled in our journey to God. We can make no further progress until we acknowledge our sin and our disobedience and commit ourselves sincerely once again to follow where He leads. But such an honest search, one that involves the will as well as the mind, cannot fail to lead us to God.

Caring for His Children

(Matthew 2:13-23)

Joseph awakened with a shudder. It was pitch black in the little mud-brick house where they had gotten temporary lodging in Bethlehem. The single window, high up on the wall, had been covered by a piece of goatskin to keep out the damp, cold winter, and the air was dead and still. A chill ran down his spine as he sat up on the little stone platform at the back of the room where the family slept. Instinctively, he reached out to touch his young bride, Mary, wrapped in a woolen cloak and lying on the mat beside him. She stirred slightly, pulled her bundled baby closer to her breast, and a few moments later Joseph could tell by her even breathing that she had returned to the sleep new mothers must glean from the few hours between feedings.

Joseph, however, was wide awake, his ears straining to pick up any unusual sounds from the darkness around him. He had been awakened by a dream, but just like the dream several months earlier which had told him of the impending birth of his son, this one, too, Joseph knew, was more than an ordinary dream. It had been vivid, and substantial—particularly real. An angel had appeared to him, telling him to rise, take the child and his mother, and flee to Egypt. Herod the king, the angel had told him, was searching for the child to destroy him.

A few days ago, this would have seemed incredible to him. Who were they, after all? An obscure peasant, trying to decide whether to stay in Bethlehem for awhile until the circumstances of his wife's pregnancy faded from the minds of his fellow townsmen so he could return to his carpenter shop in Nazareth. How could the king even be aware of their existence?

But then those Persian Magi had arrived, creating, as you can imagine, quite a stir in the little town of Bethlehem. And while their richly laden camels had waited benignly outside, they had come into the primitive little house, bearing lavish gifts of gold, frankincense, and myrrh; and they had actually bowed down and worshiped the child. Joseph could no longer sustain the comfortable myth of their anonymity. It did not seem so preposterous that word had gotten back to King Herod, and from what he knew of the king, it was entirely possible that his henchmen were on their way to Bethlehem that very night.

Herod had been on the throne in Jerusalem all Joseph's life, supported by the good graces of the Roman government. Indeed, Augustus Caesar, always uncomfortable with the unusual customs and unpredictable temperament of the Jews, was only too glad to have someone in charge who understood the people better than he and could keep things at least relatively under control. Herod flattered the emperor by building a new port city and naming it Caesarea in his honor. He also attempted to conciliate the Jews by building a lavish new temple for them.

But he taxed the people heavily, and since he was only half Jewish and appeared to have sold out to the Romans, the people never really trusted him. And Joseph knew, as did everyone else, that Herod would do anything to stay in power. At age twenty-five, when he was first appointed governor of Galilee, Herod had eliminated the resistance by smoking them and their families out of the caves in the mountains where they had taken refuge and slaughtering them all in cold blood. When he became king in 37 B.C., his first action was to execute forty-five of the most wealthy and prominent persons in the aristocratic class who opposed him. When the new high priest became too popular, Herod invited him to go swimming with some friends on a particularly hot day, and then had his friends drown the youthful priest by holding him under water as they played in the pool.

Whenever there was even a hint of opposition to his kingship, he put it down with violence and even torture. Becoming increasingly paranoid, he eventually killed his wife, whom he had apparently loved deeply, and his mother-in-law as well. And most recently, Joseph knew, he had even had his two favorite sons,

Alexander and Aristobulus, executed. Such a man, Joseph was certain, would not hesitate to murder the tiny child now cuddled in Mary's arms if he suspected even the slightest threat to his position.

A slight scuffling noise, perhaps, outside the barred door sent Joseph's heart racing. When it died away, his heart continued to pound in his ears. It seemed there was not an instant to lose. Jerusalem, after all, was only six miles away. If Herod had decided to come for his child, they could be there in less than an hour. He could not wait for morning light. Awakening his wife, Joseph hurriedly told her of the dream. Then taking a coal from among the embers of the evening's fire, he lit the oil lamp and set it on the overturned measure where it would give light to the room. He didn't want to draw any attention, but they would have to see in order to gather their few belongings and wrap them for the journey.

When their things were packed, Mary likely fed the baby while Joseph slipped outside to fetch their trusty donkey and load him up yet once again, this time for a clandestine journey into Egypt. If the donkey protested, I imagine Joseph quieted him with some extra grain. It would not do to have anyone become suspicious of their midnight escapade.

When everything was ready, Joseph snuffed out the light and the little threesome slipped through the doorway and out into the cold night air. Every scuff of the tiny donkey's hoofs echoed among the little cluster of houses in the stillness. It seemed to take an eternity, but eventually they found themselves on the highway leading south toward Hebron. Joseph had heard or seen no one, but he couldn't help looking back from time to time along the way they had come, fearful, I am sure, at every moment that the dark shapes which he took to be boulders or olive trees might turn out to be horsemen in pursuit.

By daybreak they may have covered ten miles through the rugged Hebron hills and what remained of the old oak forests. Some time that day the cold and frightened travelers would have arrived in Hebron itself, the city where Abraham had established himself some 2,000 years earlier after parting with Lot, and where David had been anointed king over Israel a millennium later. Here they would have to decide whether to continue south into the arid wastes of the Negev, or turn west and make their way to the great coastal highway which would take them south to Pelusium, the gateway to Egypt and the Nile. The temptation to take the isolated desert road may have been strong, as they must have trembled every time they were overtaken by another party along the more heavily travelled route. But for a lone couple and baby to try to brave the howling sands of the northern Sinai, especially at that time of year, would have been foolhardy, and I imagine they turned toward the coast with a prayer on their lips that God would continue to protect them as they journeyed back toward the land from which their ancestors had come so many years ago.

It would have taken them a good ten days of steady traveling to cover the 200-plus miles from Bethlehem to Egypt. Where they stayed upon their arrival we do not know. There was a very large Jewish population in Alexandria, but it seems unlikely they would have travelled that far west. Tradition says they stayed near Heliopolis, outside present-day Cairo, where the Great Pyramids had already been standing for some 2,500 years. Wherever it was, they were well out of the reach of Herod who, when he realized the Magi were not coming back to report on the new Messiah-King, sent his soldiers in a furious rage to kill all the male children in Bethlehem and throughout the entire region who were two years old or younger, just to make sure.

The brutality of that episode still sends shock waves through our otherwise idealistic images of the first Christmas. It was a cruel world then, as now, and no one was really safe. Ruthless, power-hungry men were about as likely to acknowledge the Prince of Peace in that day as their descendants are today. It has never been safe to follow Jesus Christ.

On the other hand, Herod not only failed in his objective of eliminating the competition, but things were going from bad to worse for him while Joseph and his family were away. Herod, we learn from history, contracted a particularly painful and loathsome disease which began to ulcerate his digestive system. As the disease worsened and word spread that Herod was dying, malcontents throughout his kingdom began to challenge him. Herod responded, of course, with characteristic fury. Two rabbis who stirred up a crowd to tear down an offensive eagle on the temple gate were burned alive. Another son, Antipater, was executed when Herod heard he was plotting to poison him. Fearful that no one would mourn his passing (quite a reasonable fear, I assure you), Herod collected Jewish leaders from all over the nation and locked them in the hippodrome with instructions that his archers were to massacre them upon his death so that the nation would enter a time of mourning and not just celebrate when their "beloved" king died.

Eventually the unhappy king did die in his bed in Jericho, his body convulsed with pain and his lungs no longer able to function. His successors, however, foiled his plans. They released the prisoners from the hippodrome. His final, hateful plan had miscarried, and although he did not know it, the child he had hoped to eliminate in the Bethlehem massacre was also alive and well with his parents in Egypt. Some time that spring, the angel appeared to Joseph once again, summoning him to return to Israel—Rise, take your son and your wife and go back to Israel, the angel said; and Joseph rose and took his son and his wife and went back to Israel. On his way to Judea, he heard that a last-minute change in Herod's will had placed his equally cruel and far less capable son Archelaus on the throne there, so he decided to return to his home in Nazareth in the northern district of Galilee, a place ruled now by a more even-tempered son, Herod Antipas.

Once again, God had simply and quietly accomplished his purpose despite the rantings and ravings of little men with an illusion of power. Dramatic as it may have been, this was nothing new. God has been preserving his people against all odds for thousands of years. Again and again throughout the centuries, just when it seems there is no earthly way to escape the evil intentions of the enemies of the Lord, God has delivered His people.

Christians today may find courage and comfort in God's sovereign care as well. It is worth remembering that those who seek to obey God have always had to face hostile and sometimes even violent opposition. It is not that this opposition isn't really dangerous. Of course it is. But victory for the believer has never been accomplished by force or wits. Our survival depends not on our numbers, nor on our strength, nor on a winning strategy, nor on our ability to convince or defeat the opposition. It depends today, just as it did for Joseph and his family, on our willingness to do whatever the Lord asks us to do, leaving the consequences in His hands.

Whether we are struggling with doing the right thing at work or in our marriage or in our community, whether we are struggling with anxiety about the future or the security of our family, God says, follow Me and leave the consequences in My hands. Whether you can see it or not, I am absolutely committed to care for My own. "He who dwells in the shelter of the Most High, who abides in the shadow of the Almighty, will say to the LORD, 'My refuge and my fortress; my God, in whom I trust.' For he will deliver you . . ." (Psalm 91:1-3a).

Growing Up

(Luke 2:39-52)

W ho we become depends on countless things. The lay of the land shapes us; the things we learn to fear and the things we learn to enjoy; the loved ones with whom we live. All these things shape our lives from childhood on. Our experiences and our opportunities and our history shape who we are and who we become. Our expectations and our character are shaped by the people and the circumstances that surround us.

Quite unconsciously, we begin to assume the values modeled for us by our parents and by our community. All of us are the product of that shaping process down through the years. Suffering will shape us, as will success. Many of the things which shape us will be quite beyond our control. Yet we are accountable for what we do with those forces, and for the sort of persons we become as a result. This is all part of the process of growing up, and all of us experience it.

We know very little about the boyhood years of Jesus, but clearly they had a profound impact upon the person He was becoming. They were significant years. He too was shaped by the environment, by the community in which He lived, and by the family to which He belonged. These were the most formative years of His life, yet the Scriptures are almost entirely silent about them. Virtually everything we know about nine-tenths of Jesus' life is contained in fourteen verses from the second chapter of

Luke. Yet perhaps that is enough. Set in the context of what we know about the time and the place, it may well be all we need to know. Take verses 39 and 40 (NIV), for instance:

> When Joseph and Mary had done everything required by the Law of the Lord, they returned to Galilee to their own town of Nazareth. And the child grew and became strong; he was filled with wisdom, and the grace of God was upon him.

Joseph and Mary were absolutely willing to take instruction from the Lord in the rearing and care of this child whom God had given to them. Clearly, their responsibility for Him was their first priority—they had other things to do, but their responsibility for the shaping of His life was their highest priority. Above all, they would not neglect the rituals which spelled out God's responsibility—and theirs—to join Him in a covenant which would govern and shape their lives.

Following His circumcision, the offerings at the temple, and their escape into Egypt, Joseph and Mary returned to their hometown of Nazareth in the northern province of Galilee. Without question, growing up in this unique environment would substantially affect the person Jesus was becoming.

Galilee was cut off from the rest of Israel by the great Valley of Jezreel which ran from east to west, dividing the northern and the southern parts of Palestine. Merchant caravans and invading armies had traveled that route from time immemorial. The centers of her people's culture and government had always lain farther south, however, and this rural province on the northern frontier was often under the sway of foreign rulers from as close as Syria, with its capital in Damascus, or as far away as Nineveh, headquarters of the Assyrian Empire. The population was never predominantly Jewish down through the centuries until the last century before Christ, when Aristobulus conquered the land and forcibly converted the people to Judaism. Until then it had been known as "Galilee of the nations," and it was, for all its simple, homespun atmosphere, more in touch with the real world than the intensely nationalistic provinces further south in the heart of Israel surrounding Jerusalem.

The land itself in Galilee stood in sharp contrast to the rugged, barren hills of Judea with its decaying cities. Galilee was open and bright and fresh and fertile, dotted with small, bustling communities given to the growing of olives and figs and other produce or, on the shores of the Sea of Galilee, to the commercial fishing trade. This good land with all of its richness inspired its citizens with the practical blessings of diligent labor. It was Judea which spawned philosophers and sanctioned tradition. In Galilee, one got to work with his hands, and looked a good deal more to the future than to the past.

Yet when the young boy, Jesus, climbed to the peak of the hill south of Nazareth, He could easily see Mount Tabor standing all by itself in the midst of the plain, from whose striking heights Deborah and Barak had stormed down to fall upon the Canaanites in the plain of Megiddo. He could also appreciate the strategy of Gideon as his handful of men occupied the heights surrounding the vast Midianite army during the night, throwing them into confusion within a deceptive circle of fire and noise. Not far off He could see the heights of Gilboa, where Israel's first king, Saul, had lost his life in a disastrous battle with the Philistines. And whenever He climbed up to the pinnacles surrounding His community, I am sure He spent time reflecting on the paths that had shaped His people and His culture. Tales of the great armies of Egypt and Assyria which had passed along the broad valley just to the south of Nazareth, lent credibility to the prophecies of the great battle of Armageddon which would be fought here between the forces of good and evil in the Last Days. All these grand things must have woven themselves together in the mind and spirit of this lad Jesus during the days He was growing up in Nazareth in Galilee.

Without question, Jesus would have heard many tales about His ancestors and their place in the land. All of this would have shaped His self-image, His understanding of who He was, and His expectations for who He would become. And there would have been a certain security, founded not only on His parent's love and His father's place in the community, but on the extended family and the many relations which surrounded them. As He grew old enough to venture out on His own, I imagine Jesus probably hiked through the old oak forests on the mountains of Galilee where His father felled timber, and then down, after the better part of a day's journey, into the tropical landscape which surrounded the blue jewel of the Lake of Gennesaret, where His uncle Zebedee and his wife Salome (Mary's sister) ran a fishing business. Jesus always seemed to be at ease around boats, and I imagine He often went out on the lake with His uncle and His cousins, James and John, as they worked the family business together.

Jesus, of course, was learning His family's business as well. His father was a carpenter, but most of us fail to realize what a demanding job this was. We usually imagine Joseph and His son in their little shop, finishing furniture, which they certainly did. But they also would have built houses. In those days, houses were constructed of huge timbers, felled in the surrounding forests, and shaped into beams by primitive hand tools. It took two men with a ribbon saw to cut through the trunk. Then, after hauling the great oak logs down from the surrounding hills, Jesus would have had to help His father square them into beams by chopping at them with a crude tool called an adz, or sawing their length with a hand saw—either way a very difficult task.

Constructing doors, window lattices, and locks for buildings was also demanding work, and special skill was required to shape tables, chests, wheels, and a variety of tools for the craftsmen of the area. Somehow history has always pictured Jesus as a fragile, contemplative person, but He was almost certainly the opposite. Carpentry demanded uncommon strength and practicality, and Jesus would have had to become tough and muscular in order to accomplish what was expected of Him in that job.

Thus we are not surprised when the Bible tells us that Jesus grew and became strong. If you are only going to choose a few words to describe this man, they must be significant words, and here was a man who showed great strength. Living the sort of life they lived was physically demanding, but Jesus grew physically to meet the demands.

Nevertheless, there was more to Jesus than mere physical strength and practical expertise. He was a thoughtful and intelligent boy and His parents must have noticed early on the uncommon wisdom and insight He began to display. Education began in the home for all Jewish children under the direction of the mother for the first three years, but from age three on, primary responsibility fell to the father to begin teaching the Law and ultimately to teach his son a trade. Education was essentially religious education, directed at helping the child understand the most important things about life. In understanding the nature of God through what He had done and through what He required in the Law, children could come to understand who He was, the One who had formed them, and what His purposes were. What could be more essential than that, the heart of their education? No doubt Deuteronomy 6, with its emphasis upon the nature of God and the responsibility of parents to teach their children how to love and serve Him, occupied a prominent place in the home of Joseph and Mary.

By the age of six, Jesus would have gone to spend part of His day with a teacher from the local synagogue, where He would sit with other children on a mat in a semi-circle around the elderly instructor and recite passages from the Law and the prophets and the Psalms. He would also practice writing the letters He had begun to learn at home on a little wooden tablet with wax. While the education undergone by most children was relatively informal, it was astonishingly effective. By the time He was a young man, Jesus apparently knew four languages. He knew His native Hebrew; the Aramaic language spoken by His contemporaries; the Latin used by the Roman occupational government; and the Greek which was the predominant language of commerce and inter-cultural activity.

But what most impressed those who encountered Jesus during this time was the tremendous perception and insight into life which He had gained from the Scriptures. The Holy Scriptures were central to His home life, and obviously were the heart and soul of His education.

In addition to studying the Law, all devout Jews celebrated the history of their people through participating in the great feasts which God had established as memorials of His significant acts in history. It was during one of these celebrations, in fact, that a singular incident took place which seemed to be particularly revealing as to the person Jesus was becoming—so significant that it becomes the only thing we hear about Him from this period of time.

Jesus was just twelve years old. It was the year before what we would call His "bar-mitzvah," when He would officially become a man. Perhaps in anticipation of this great milestone, and in order to help prepare Him for it, Jesus' parents took Him with them to the Feast of the Passover which they attended every year in Jerusalem. Not everyone went to the Passover Feast every year. It is an indication of Mary and Joseph's commitment that they made that two-week round trip every year to be a part of the festivities of their people, to renew their commitment to the God who had delivered their ancestors from slavery in Egypt, and who promised them deliverance.

But this particular year, after the festivities were over, they had a very startling experience with their son—this young boy, who had always been a model of obedience, disappeared. Since they were traveling in a large group, they didn't notice until the end of the first day's journey back toward the north, about twenty miles. Then, not finding Him among their relatives and friends and frantic with concern, they took the next day to travel back to the city of Jerusalem, and there spent most of a third day looking for Him, perhaps checking in with relatives and friends with whom He might have stayed after becoming separated from His family.

Ultimately, they found Him in the temple compound, under one of the porticoes where the great rabbis and teachers of the Law often gathered to share informal teaching and discussion of the Law with the common people. There they found their young son, utterly engaged in the discussions, listening to the teachers and asking questions which showed such profound insight that everyone who heard Him was amazed. Undoubtedly, Jesus had become the unconscious center of attention as He engaged the elders of His people in dialogue which drew them to the heart of the meaning and application of the laws of God.

To understand this incident and Jesus' parents' reaction to it (as well as Jesus' response to them), we have to understand something about the nature of the incarnation which has always been something of a mystery to us. Jesus was not born knowing He was God and understanding the nature of the universe. He had to develop and grow and learn just like anyone else. That is why His experience parallels ours. He had questions and doubts and temptations just as we do. How He came to fully understand His divine nature is a mystery which continues to intrigue theologians two thousand years later. But it seems to me that this incident is particularly revealing in this regard.

It is likely that Mary had taken the young Jesus aside in preparation for this momentous visit to the Holy City and told Him once again about the remarkable events and prophecies which had led up to and surrounded His birth. Life since then apparently had been quite normal, but Mary never lost sight of the future which had been predicted by angels and prophets; and of course, she had never forgotten the miracle of Jesus' conception and birth. Chances are she suggested that He needed to take this Passover very seriously as He prepared for the big day that next year in His own life. Yet Mary really didn't understand what was happening.

For Jesus, on the other hand, things were finally beginning to make sense. All those passages in the prophets which He had read and reflected upon all those years, all those expectations embodied in the Law, seemed to be pointing to Him in some mysterious way. He must have had a tremendous sense of the way in which God had even brought Him into existence and was shaping His life for this moment. Had He been much older than twelve when this all began to fit together in His mind, there might have been a temptation not to take it very seriously. As we get older, we become much too jaded to take those kinds of things seriously. But as it was, in His innocence and the purity of His heart at that young age, He concluded that this is what His mother had been trying to tell Him when she was preparing Him for the Passover. Thus He was quite honestly surprised when she reprimanded Him for His thoughtless disregard of their feelings.

"Why were you searching for me?" He asked. "Didn't you know I had to be in my Father's house?" You can just hear Him— "You are the ones who told me all about this. Why didn't you understand where I would be and what I would be doing?" They, of course, were dumbfounded by this reply, and Jesus soon realized that this was a mystery too profound to expect even those who were closest to Him to understand. So without further hesitation, He accompanied them back to Nazareth where He willingly submitted Himself to their authority. Part of being about His heavenly Father's business was to place Himself entirely at the disposal of His earthly family. And that Jesus did without argument or complaint.

Though she did not understand, none of this escaped Mary's attention. She continued to treasure this incredible experience in her heart. The account of Jesus' boyhood concludes with the summary statement that "Jesus grew in wisdom and stature, and in favor with God and men." Not only did He grow strong and intelligent, but He became wise in His application of that knowledge. Both God and His fellow men found His character and conduct to be extremely appealing as they saw in this young man the precise shaping of the image of God. Jesus was growing up, just as He ought.

We should not fool ourselves into thinking that this was easy for Jesus. We are told later in Hebrews that Jesus was tempted in every way, just as we are. That means that in some way He had to do battle with lust and pride and anger, just as we do. The difference is, He was successful. And the result was the most beautiful person who ever lived. You just couldn't help being impressed with His rugged strength, His wonderful sensitivity and insight, and with the beauty of a life lived wholly as God intended.

It is significant that Jesus' life predominately was shaped by parents who loved Him deeply and who took specific steps to nurture Him in the ways of the Lord. He had to learn how to get along in a family. The Bible tells us elsewhere that Jesus had four brothers and several sisters. All kinds of things go on in a family with that many children, and Jesus had to learn how to deal with the family dynamics. Unquestionably, the wealth of wisdom contained in the Word of God was central to the conversation of that family. They took the instruction of Deuteronomy 6 seriously. It was central to their education and to practical, everyday living. They spent time together learning the stories of their people and how their lives were affected by the obedience or disobedience of their ancestors. Jesus was expected to work hard and pull his weight within the family. Life wasn't easy and He had to participate. He was required to act sensitively and responsibly toward other members of the family. The fact that He was unique did not stop His mother from challenging Him when she thought He had stepped out of line. And even that reprimand, though it was undeserved, is instructive to us concerning the environment that shaped Jesus' life.

Jesus also was given plenty of exposure to the world God had created, and I can't help but think that His parents constantly nurtured His appreciation for that world. As you listen to His teaching later on, He is always talking about the birds or the flowers, something He is appreciating in nature, the way a seed grows and becomes a plant and is finally harvested. He saw God's hand in all of that. As they walked the highways and byways of Palestine, they spoke of the God who had made it all and His purposes in doing so. I imagine had Jesus and His family lived in the city instead of in the country, they would have pointed out similar things about the urban environment and would have taken every opportunity they could to get out into the countryside. They did travel an extraordinary amount, especially considering the hazards of travel in those days.

His family also made certain that Jesus participated in the corporate religious activities of their people. I am not sure we all take this very seriously! But Joseph and Mary knew those activities were profoundly significant, and it would not do to neglect them. They were not like "enlightened parents" today who think it best to let their children decide whether they would rather spend Sunday morning in bed, or earn extra money. They knew they could give their children no greater asset than knowing the Lord. They knew they had the responsibility as parents to shape their children in the way of the Lord, exposing them to the rituals and the history and the direction that God had given to their people.

Nor would it be true to assume their son would not have to face the sorts of temptations young people face today. If you read between the lines you can see it clearly—all sorts of people drank too much, or stole from one another, or lived sexually promiscuous lives. But Jesus' parents obviously made it clear how destructive such behavior was, and provided in their home life such an attractive alternative that Jesus never found such activity appealing.

It is important to recognize that it takes today, just as it took

2,000 years ago, a specific, conscious, dedicated effort to raise our children "in the nurture and admonition of the Lord." Each generation is shaped by the forces which surround it. But no generation is simply at the mercy of forces beyond its control. The victim mentality which marks our culture today does us all a profound disservice. We are victims only of our own short-sightedness and lack of discipline. God has given us a significant responsibility to shape the next generation within a world which offers both promise and peril. He has also given us the resources to accomplish this. It is the most important responsibility any generation is ever given.

Baptized by His Spirit

(Matthew 3:13-17)

W e'll call his name Menehem, because for as long as he could remember he had been blessed (or cursed) with a sensitive, penitent spirit such as his name implied. Even in his early teens he genuinely grieved over the sinfulness which seemed to well up almost involuntarily from deep within his soul. As a young man he carried with him a sense of responsibility for the sins of his countrymen—indeed, for the sins of the whole world. His neighbors in the tiny village of Bethany on the eastern slope of the Mount of Olives, just two miles from Jerusalem, considered him a good and compassionate man, if a bit melancholy. But inside it seemed to Menehem that the forces of good and evil were doing battle for his soul, and that despite his best intentions he was always giving the advantage to the forces of evil.

This particular morning he left his home early, cresting the brow of the Mount of Olives before sunrise and slipping down into the dark valley known as the Kidron below the city walls. Hurrying up the steep slopes of the temple mount, he had turned into the temple courtyard through the Sheep Gate below the austere-looking Antonia Fortress in time for the morning sacrifice. Often it seemed to him that the priests were hurrying mindlessly through a ritual which had lost its meaning for them; but somehow the innocent bleating of the sheep always sent pangs of remorse through his sensitive soul, and the pain had a purging effect that helped him through the day.

In Solomon's portico, he met the others who would be traveling with him that day, and they headed back out through the city gates, descending once again into the Kidron Valley. This time, however, they branched off to the left, passing to the north of the Mount of Olives on the road to Jericho. Menehem hardly knew his traveling companions, and from time to time he would lag behind, lost in thought; but it would be foolhardy to travel this route alone. It was notorious for robbers who concealed themselves in the deep ravines, from which they would emerge suddenly to attack unwary travelers.

The road from Jerusalem to Jericho was steep, descending some 3,000 feet in a little over twelve miles, and following roughly the route of the Wadi Qilt, a tremendous gorge carved out of the barren Jerusalem hills by winter torrents. For about three hours, as the sun climbed into the sky, Menehem and his friends wound their way along the valley floor, littered with rock and debris. It seemed to him somehow analogous to his own life, barren and unpromising, the more so the farther he wandered from the heart that beat at the core of his people on Mount Zion. For all his sensitivity, he had to admit he was no better than his fathers, who had so consistently wandered off down desolate byways, ignoring the gracious hand of God. He could recite the whole of Psalm 106, cataloging God's historic acts of mercy and intervention on behalf of his people, even as his forefathers turned away time and again. "Both we and our fathers have sinned," he quoted quietly as the barren wasteland fell away behind him, "we have committed iniquity, we have done wickedly. . . . Many times he delivered them, but they were rebellious in their purposes, and were brought low through their iniquity." He continued reciting the psalm, "Save us, O LORD our God, and gather us from among the nations, that we may give thanks to thy holy name and glory in thy praise."

He yearned for that deliverance from the imprisonment of sin. That was why he was traveling now, down toward the Jordan River which writhed through the Great Rift Valley on its tortured route to the Dead Sea. He had heard there was a revival going on there, centered on the powerful preaching of a man they had begun to call "John the Baptizer," a man who was not afraid to call even the scribes and Pharisees to repentance. The people who had heard him reported there was something compelling about the man and his message, yet Menehem was skeptical. Would things really ever change? The prophet Jeremiah, another man with a sensitive conscience, had proclaimed, "The heart is deceitful above all things, and desperately corrupt; who can understand it?" and Menehem agreed. The heart of mankind—his own heart—seemed bound to sin, no matter how much one might long for change. Sin held the human heart with such a tenacious grip. Like the road on which they walked, life seemed like one long, barren, dusty pathway toward disappointment and death.

Suddenly, Menehem realized that his companions had stopped. They had just rounded a bend in the road, and he looked up to see that the gorge along which they had been traveling had opened up to reveal a spectacular view of the Jordan valley some two miles away, and perhaps 500 feet below them. At his feet lay stretched a bright green forest, teeming with life, fed by the springs which had supported a colony at Jericho in the midst of a desert land for over 7,000 years already, one of the oldest cities in the world.

The beauty and vitality of the scene lifted his spirits, and the words of Isaiah sprang to his mind:

The wilderness and the dry land shall be glad, the desert shall rejoice and blossom. . . . Then the eyes of the blind shall be opened, and the ears of the deaf unstopped; then shall the lame man leap like a hart, and the tongue of the dumb sing for joy. For waters shall break forth in the wilderness, and streams in the desert (Isaiah 35:1, 5-6).

There they were—waters breaking forth in the wilderness and streams in the desert, "And the ransomed of the LORD shall return, and come to Zion with singing; everlasting joy shall be upon their heads; they shall obtain joy and gladness, and sorrow and sighing shall flee away."

Menehem had had enough of sorrow and sighing, and he longed for that joy. Maybe God could change a man's heart after all. Maybe Ezekiel was right when he prophesied:

A new heart I will give you, and a new spirit I will put within you; and I will take out of your flesh the heart of stone and give you a heart of flesh. And I will put my spirit within you, and cause you to walk in my statutes and be careful to observe my ordinances (Ezekiel 36:26-27).

That's what it would take, he knew: a new spirit to replace a heart of stone. Was it possible that this John was even the Messiah toward whom all those wonderful prophecies pointed? If so, then anything was possible!

Menehem and his friends hurried on down the valley; he didn't even want to stop in Jericho. Hope had refreshed his soul after the long journey through the desert, and now he couldn't wait to get to the Jordan River, where they had learned John was baptizing that day. When they finally clambered down the banks of the river through the thick vegetation, Menehem was transfixed by what he saw. A man not far from his own age, but weathered by the desert sun, strode back and forth on the river bank, his voice now echoing across the water, now dropping to an intense whisper. He seemed oblivious to the sensation created by his preaching. It was, Menehem thought, as though the voice of God Himself had stirred to life from somewhere deep in John's soul. He had read many times in the Scriptures the words, "Thus saith the LORD . . ." penned by the prophets, but here that phrase seemed somehow believable and compelling. If this was not the Messiah, it was certainly a prophet, breaking the silence of 400 years in Israel!

"I baptize you with water for repentance," John was saying,

but he who is coming after me is mightier than I, whose sandals I am not worthy to carry; he will baptize you with the Holy Spirit and with fire. His winnowing fork is in his hand, and he will clear his threshing floor and gather his wheat into the granary, but the chaff he will burn with unquenchable fire (Matthew 3:11-12).

Even now, John concluded, the kingdom of heaven is at hand!

The words resonated with the voice of all the great prophets of Israel. Like Malachi, they had often warned that the Day of the

Lord would involve a purging fire—but that, Menehem thought, was most appropriate. Knowing the depth of his own sin, he did not doubt that any real change could come about only when the chaff had truly been consumed. There was plenty of chaff in his own soul that needed to be consumed. He was disappointed by the revelation that John was not the promised Messiah who would baptize with the Holy Spirit. He didn't know how long he would have to wait for that, but such a thought could not detain him now. He knew he wanted desperately to be cleansed, to be washed from his sin, to be made whole and fresh and clean and new.

John had finished speaking and had waded out into the river, inviting any who had truly repented of their sin to come and receive his baptism. Before he knew it, Menehem was on his knees in the river before the Baptizer, weeping and asking God to touch his tarnished spirit and to renew it. John had placed his hand on Menehem's shoulder and was pouring water over his head. "In the name of Yahweh, you are forgiven. Go and sin no more."

For a long time, Menehem sat on the shore, watching the simple ritual repeated again and again for scores of his fellow Israelites. He *did* feel forgiven, deep down inside, and he wanted to savor the feeling. In fact, what he wanted was to know that this feeling of newness and wholeness might continue indefinitely. After all, this was not the first time he had confessed his sins and sought God's forgiveness. But he wanted more than forgiveness; he wanted to be healed. He wanted to be healed in his soul. In the depths of his soul he wanted to be made new. He wanted more than anything else in the world, he realized, to have his spirit renewed. Did he dare to believe that this was the time? Could that transformation of his spirit for which he longed begin here, this time, with this repentance, at this moment? Desperately he feared that this renewal might be just like all the others, that by the time he got back to Bethany, the novelty might have worn off and the world would be as bleak as ever.

The crowd was thinning and the sun had lowered over the Jerusalem hills beyond the Jordan valley when Menehem became aware that something was happening. The noise of the people around John had suddenly quieted, and when he looked, he saw an expression of awe and excitement in John's eyes which he had not seen before, like the look you might see in a child's eyes on Christmas morning! Menehem turned to follow his gaze, and now he felt a shiver of excitement himself, though he didn't know why. John was watching the approach of a man who walked with long, easy strides and a natural confidence which seemed to suggest he was at home in the world, and yet at the same time that he had no attachment to it.

A moment before, John had been the man in charge, but now he was scrambling up the riverbank toward the newcomer with a childlike eagerness that piqued the interest of every observer. When they met, Menehem saw the two men grasp each other by the shoulders. He was too far away to hear what they were saying, but he heard the new man laugh and he thought he had never heard a sound so delightful and so liberating in all his life. There was nothing self-conscious about it, nothing forced. It seemed to come from a great and pure spirit, to which Menehem was immediately drawn.

They had started moving toward the river again, but John seemed to be protesting. When they had come near to where he was standing, the man turned to John once more, grasped him by the shoulders, and said, "Let it be so now; it is proper for us to do this to fulfill all righteousness." John shrugged his shoulders and turned down toward the water. As they walked past Menehem, the man looked at him with eyes that seemed to see all the way into his soul, and yet, much to his surprise, seemed not to condemn him for what they saw. Perhaps all the ugly things Menehem knew seemed to take up residence in his soul had actually been washed away by John's baptism. In any case, he couldn't imagine that this man needed to have anything washed away. The expression on his face was so open and unapologetic. That must have been the cause of John's protest. Whoever this man was, Menehem had no categories to describe him. Certainly he was a man different from any man Mehehem had known.

He watched, again transfixed as the man knelt before John, and John, still hesitant, poured water over his bowed head. If you asked Menehem what happened next, he would be hard pressed to tell you. He only knew that in all his years of reading and meditating about God, he had never in his life felt closer to God than he did in those moments. In fact, he was seized with an impression of God's presence in that very place. It was frightening and exhilarating at the same time, and suddenly he knew that this must be the man about whom all the prophets up to and including John had spoken! This was the servant Isaiah had written about, the One who would, in some way in His body, bear the sins of the world. This must be why He was receiving the baptism of John, though He seemed not to deserve it or need it.

John would later describe seeing the heavens open and the Spirit of God descending like a dove and resting on this man, and then hearing a voice from heaven saying, "This is my Son, whom I love; with him I am well pleased." This, the Baptizer would tell his followers excitedly, is what he had been talking about all along. This is what his ministry was all about. This was the direction he had been pointing. This was the One whom John had come into the world to reveal, the One who had come into the world to baptize believers with the Holy Spirit and with fire.

Menehem could believe it. This was the man who would turn his heart of stone into a heart of flesh; this was the man who would put a new Spirit in him which would enable him from his heart to walk in the way of the Lord. What he had hoped and prayed for all his life had finally come to be.

⟨⟩

The fact is, of course, this was truer than Menehem or any other observer could possibly have understood at that moment. For Jesus' baptism did introduce the remarkable new thing that God had promised to do on this earth, namely, the radical transformation of sinful men and women by means of the indwelling Holy Spirit. John's baptism had been preparatory but not complete. It had been a baptism of repentance, but now John saw the Holy Spirit descend on this man. And while Jesus is the archetype of this—the man in whom the whole fullness of God dwelt bodily, as they could see—he establishes for us what God intends for us to be, as well. For you and I also are created to be men and women in the image of God, fully and powerfully reflecting Him through the indwelling power of His Holy Spirit.

This is what sets Christianity apart from every other religion. All other religions have their advice and instructions on how to live. But they fall short at this critical point: What good is advice if we are incapable of following it? Christianity alone begins by offering to change our hearts, and proceeds by equipping us from within to become the sort of people God calls us to be, through the working of His Holy Spirit.

This, then, was the moment God chose to introduce his Son Jesus to a world that desperately needed the Messiah. They could not have fully understood what was taking place. But in his baptism were represented the essential elements of new life for all of us. It won't even begin without a genuinely penitent heart, and we will no doubt spend a lifetime cultivating that spirit. But if we are walking with Jesus, we will be so caught up in Him we will hardly notice the time and the energy, for we will begin to know the delight of that spring welling up within us for eternal life.

Temptation and Desire

(Matthew 4:1-11)

As Jesus left the Jordan River and climbed into the barren hills which marked the ragged edges of the Rift Valley, He knew down deep in His soul that a time of testing lay ahead of Him. His ministry was beginning. The audience had gathered; the strains of the opening overture were still echoing down the labyrinth of the Jordan Valley; and now the curtain had risen on a great cosmic drama which would move from scene to scene with growing intensity, compelling Him forward through heights of dizzying success and depths of desolating anguish to the grand *denouement* of history!

By now, Jesus could easily recognize the voice of His Father's Spirit. He knew that, like Moses at Mount Sinai, He was being called upon to go into the wilderness in preparation for the tremendous things which lay ahead. In fact, He would face there a time of testing more severe than anything He had faced to date. God was not leading Him into temptation, but into the wilderness, where He would be tempted by the devil.

It is possible that each of us will have a "wilderness" experience which shapes us, for better or for worse. For Jesus, this was a literal wilderness. The hills above the Jordan are desolate and forbidding. He was alone, with the exception of the wild animals, as Mark reminds us. And indeed, there were lions and other wild beasts lurking there. But Jesus would face a more formidable foe in the person of Satan himself. Whether he came to Jesus in a personal form, or whether he haunted his dreams at midnight, the reality of his presence would be overwhelming and terrible, and Jesus would have to deal with it.

We don't know precisely how Jesus occupied His time during this ordeal, whether He moved from place to place or whether He found a spot to be alone with God the Father. We do know that He fasted there forty days and forty nights.

Throughout history, fasting has been a central spiritual discipline. It is a way of exercising control over the bodily appetites and desires which normally control us. In addition, fasting cleanses our bodies from a build-up of toxins which normally numb our perceptions, with the result that, after a significant fast, our awareness of life and of spiritual things is heightened and intensified. So, like Moses and Elijah before Him, Jesus had determined that this was the appropriate way for Him also to begin His ministry. It would serve many purposes:

- To humble himself before God
- To devote Himself to communion with God
- To separate Himself from worldly distractions
- To sharpen His spiritual sensitivity and perception
- To bring His natural appetites under control
- To test His ability to deal with adversity
- To prepare Himself for the great adventure upon which He was being launched.

Like those who had gone through such an ordeal before Him, Jesus anticipated that He would emerge from the desert a "new man," specially equipped by His experience for the Father's service.

You might wonder whether a person can actually go without food for forty days (sometimes forty minutes seems too long!) Recent news reports described how a young man survived forty-three days, lost in the Himalayas, with no food but a single bar of chocolate. The fact is, fourty days is about the maximum time a healthy body can go without food. Most of the physical symptoms we associate with not eating—the hunger pangs, headaches, and dizziness—are over within the first ten days. For the next few weeks one actually cares little for food, and mind and spirit are sharpened by that cleansing of our bodies. But after about forty-days, the body has consumed all its reserves and begins to draw on living tissue. That is when starvation begins. At this time one is overwhelmed by ravenous hunger.

This is the stage to which Jesus had come when "the tempter" came to confront Him. I find it fascinating and informative that Satan apparently so miscalculated what was happening to Jesus. It was absolutely true that Jesus was at His most vulnerable moment physically; but at the same time, He had been directing all His attention to communion with the Father and must have been stronger than ever spiritually.

I think it is a fact that Satan cannot fully comprehend the things of the Spirit. We think of him as a formidable adversary, and he is. But he is not quite up to speed on what is involved in spiritual things. He concentrates his attention on the material things which certainly distract us, and when we live our lives out pretty much in the material world, he is very successful at challenging us. But those who are filled with God's Spirit actually have a tremendous advantage in dealing with Satan, if we will use it.

So the tempter came to Jesus when He was ravenously hungry and said, "If you are the Son of God, command these stones to become loaves of bread." You can hear the derision in his voice, challenging those words which had been so encouraging at Jesus' baptism, where the Father had said, "You are my beloved Son, with you I am well pleased." Satan is about to tempt Him to test this statement: Is it really true? Are you truly the Son of God?

Satan makes it clear he doesn't believe it for a moment. Essentially he says, "Prove it! This should be a simple enough thing for you. The Son of God should have unlimited powers, after all. Prove who you are by turning these stones into loaves of bread." Obviously, he wants to capitalize on Jesus' ravenous hunger. You and I, who think we will starve when we miss a meal, have no terms by which to measure the strength of this temptation.

But its greatest strength is in its subtlety. It seems such an innocuous thing. He is not being tempted to do something extreme or immoral. What could be more innocent than providing bread for a hungry man? But you see, Jesus was being tempted as we often are to turn His legitimate power to His own advantage, and such an act would have distorted His power irreparably. Had Jesus chosen to serve Himself, this would have shown distrust for His heavenly Father's care.

It is very significant that this temptation so closely parallels the most famous temptation in all history. What was it that Satan had tempted Adam and Eve to do? Eat some fruit, that's all! That episode seemed pretty innocuous, as well. Would God begrudge them a bite to eat? Would God begrudge His Son a bite to eat?

But, of course, there was something far more important happening below the surface. Adam and Eve had a unique place and position, with unique and dazzling powers. They had been made in the very image of God, with an ability unlike anything else in all creation to make free choices and thus to determine their own destiny. The question was, would they exercise this awesome power under the direction of God's divine authority? Or would they seize that power and turn it to their own advantage?

We all know what they did; they chose the latter and brought devastation and dishonor upon the whole human race. Now the question was: how would the second Adam, Jesus, deal with essentially the same temptation?

While the first Adam had every conceivable advantage—he was not hungry, all his needs were being met, he was surrounded by many appealing and legitimate alternatives in a place of abundance and beauty—the second Adam had none of those advantages. He was famished and there was nothing at all to satisfy His hunger in this barren wilderness. The temptation was very real. Would God really mind if He turned these stones into bread? Jesus responds in verse 4:

> It is written, "Man shall not live by bread alone, but by every word that proceeds from the mouth of God."

It is the perfect quote, and demonstrates Jesus' intimate familiarity with the Scriptures. Taken from Deuteronomy 8, the context is Moses' reminder to the children of Israel of how God had cared for them and fed them with manna in the wilderness for forty years (not just forty days) when there was no apparent means of keeping them alive. In fact, Moses reminded them, their hunger was a test to see "what was in [their] heart, whether [they] would keep his commandments or not." He ultimately taught them that they are not sustained by an adequate supply of bread, but, even in that wilderness, by the will and purpose of God. He speaks and it comes to pass. God says, "Let the earth put forth vegetation, plants yielding seed, and fruit trees bearing fruit . . ." and it happens. It is the word that proceeds from the mouth of God that provides for us. That is why Jesus reminds us we need not be anxious about material things. Our needs will be met if we "seek first the kingdom of God and His righteousness."

Jesus knew (as every believer should know) that He could abandon Himself to the Father's care, for the Father was in fact the only true source for meeting all His needs. He need not manipulate His power to His own advantage, for God had undertaken for Him. He could obey God with a reckless abandon because He trusted Him. Jesus saw through to the heart of Satan's deceit. He knew He could trust His Father without reservation. He had successfully deflected the devil's first temptation.

But Satan is a master at his craft. He saw the great trust which Jesus had for His Father and knew he could not overpower it by a direct assault. So, like a master at judo or jujitsu, where one uses his opponent's superior strength against him, Satan immediately shifts his ground and tries to use the momentum of Jesus' strong response to throw Him off balance.

"Oh, so you trust your Father, do you?" says Satan in effect. "Well, then you won't mind proving it, will you!" This time he accompanies Jesus to the highest point on the temple wall, probably the roof edge of Herod's royal portico, overhanging the deep ravine of the Kidron Valley which looked down some 450 feet to the rocky floor of the valley below. It was an awesome and spectacular spot. Tradition says Jesus' brother James was thrown off the wall near this point some years later—a martyr for his steadfast belief in the Christ.

Here Satan confronts Jesus once again, "If you are the Son of God," he says,

[then] throw yourself down; for it is written, "He will give his angels charge of you" and "On their hands they will bear you up, lest you strike your foot against a stone."

That might seem like an outlandish temptation, but it is a reasonable one for Satan to try at this point. He is saying, "You say you trust your heavenly Father to care for you and that is why you will not turn your powers to your own advantage. Fine. That's very commendable—if it's true. You could demonstrate this trust by quite literally abandoning yourself to His care, as you have just said you are willing to do. If you are truly His Son, He will not let you fall to your death. Show me that you truly believe it. Do you have the courage to throw yourself down? To risk everything on His promises? You have made some pretty great claims, Jesus. Are you really willing to risk everything on His promises? Surely you will not shrink from demonstrating your trust and your Father's trustworthiness?"

Satan believed he had Jesus in a kind of "catch 22" here—certainly He cannot refuse to do Satan's bidding now without appearing to doubt the promises of God. To make his trap appear all the more legitimate, Satan quotes the magnificent ninety-first Psalm, which is filled with promises of God's care. It begins:

He who dwells in the shelter of the Most High, who abides in the shadow of the Almighty, will say to the LORD, "My refuge and my fortress; my God, in whom I trust." For he will deliver you from the snare of the fowler. . .

The psalm proceeds to talk about hazard after hazard encountered by God's child, and consistently promises that God will deliver him.

Will Jesus be tempted to prove His trust with such a rash act? Once again, Jesus responds with a wonderfully appropriate text from Scripture, from Deuteronomy 6:16. He says simply, "You shall not put the LORD your God to the test." In that passage Moses is referring to a time in the wilderness where the people were trying to provoke God into doing what they wanted done. Complaining that He had not really cared for them as He ought, they asked, "Is Yahweh among us or not?" They were trying to provoke Him to do what they wanted Him to do, to get Him to prove Himself by responding to their complaints.

But God never bargains with us. He does not need to prove Himself. He asks of us as He asked of them, that we obey His commandments and that we do what is right and good. For Jesus to try to force His hand with some dramatic act would have been most inappropriate. God's care was promised to those who simply obeyed Him. The whole of Psalm 91 was directed to such persons. Jesus was quite willing simply to obey and leave the results in God's hands. He had no doubt that God would ultimately prove trustworthy.

Jesus knows the only thing the Father asks of Him is a quiet, confident obedience. If He is willing to do what His Father has called Him to do, then He can rest in Him. God is under no obligation to prove Himself with spectacular miracles or with a guarantee of health or wealth to His children. He asks us simply to obey.

Jesus had deflected the second temptation and Satan now staked everything on one last, desperate attempt. Casting aside all subtlety, he said to Jesus, I tell you what: I will give you all the kingdoms of the world "if you will fall down and worship me." Now, Jesus knew that the kingdoms of the earth were not really Satan's to give. Nevertheless, He also knew that they could only be purchased at a great price, the price of His own experience of the wrath of God against sin. This was Satan's offer to step aside and concede the great struggle for the minds and hearts of the world, if Jesus would recognize his place and his authority.

We could not fault Jesus for wondering if there were any alternatives. Was it possible in any way to reach His goal without the desperate anguish of the cross? Even if this appeal of Satan's was exposed as fraudulent, it would introduce the idea of a possible alternative to enduring the wrath of God. And how many times have we allowed ourselves to be deceived because we so desperately wanted something to be true? Just perhaps, Satan could deflect Jesus from His goal.

But Jesus' response once again is immediate: "Begone, Satan!

for it is written, 'You shall worship the Lord your God and him only shall you serve.'" Jesus refuses to contemplate any alternatives to doing God's will. "Him only shall you serve. His word only shall you obey." That is the only word that I need, Jesus says, to instruct Me and give direction to My life. God's way is the only way. And then He exercises His God-given authority to dismiss Satan. "Begone," He says.

You and I are almost surprised when Satan leaves so easily, though in fact God's Word offers us the same power. James 4:7,8 says, "Resist the devil and he will flee from you. Draw near to God and he will draw near to you." When Jesus does this, the response is immediate. As the final verse of our text reveals, "Then the devil left him, and behold, angels came and ministered to him."

We could learn a great deal from the way in which the Master dealt with temptation. In the first place, He was able to recognize deception because He was so intimately familiar with the Scriptures. If we are not, sooner or later we will be deceived. Secondly, Jesus set an example by responding to each temptation immediately. We play with temptation for a while, and the longer we do so, the greater its power over us becomes.

But the other thing we may learn from Jesus' experience has to do with the subtle nature of temptation. The word itself conjures images of demons urging us to do horrible things. But the nature of Jesus' temptation was that He was urged to believe He could receive a good thing by way of a bad act. That is precisely what Adam and Eve were tempted to do. The Bible tells us that when they saw "the tree was good for food, and that it was a delight to the eyes, and that the tree was to be desired to make one wise"— all good things—they chose to disobey God in the pursuit of a good goal.

Most of our sins are of the same nature. We seek pleasure, or security, or wisdom, or reputation, or relief from distress—all good things—but the temptation is to take our own shortcuts instead of following God's good path. And the end can only be disastrous. Truly, good things come only from the hand of our God.

To Open the Eyes That Are Blind

(Luke 4:14-30)

Jesus emerged from the wilderness with a focus and a vitality which would stun His fellow countrymen. It was time for His ministry to begin and He would launch it in His native Galilee. But Jesus was under no illusion concerning how His message would be received. On the one hand, these people had spent a lifetime listening to their rabbis drone on in the synagogues, speculating about the possible application of the law. These good folks had dutifully attended the solemn assemblies in the temple where priests and Levites trudged blankly through the ritual of a dozen centuries. Now they would be confronted with a man who spoke with authority and conviction, a man who brought them the Word of God with freshness and vitality, a man who knew the relevance of faith and demonstrated it with power. But the very power and freshness of His message would be a serious threat to the status quo.

We see the drama begin to unfold as Jesus arrives at the synagogue in His native village of Nazareth on the Sabbath day. Here would be the great challenge to His teaching, for not only were these people steeped in tradition, they were sure they already knew Jesus.

The synagogues had grown up during the Exile in the absence of any center for worship and sacrifice, the temple having been destroyed and the people dispersed. Every Sabbath day, the people would gather to hear the Scriptures expounded and to be reminded of God's expectations for them. The service was very simple and straightforward. After the men had gathered in the main sanctuary and the women had entered by the rear door to sit in the gallery, the service would begin, perhaps with the singing of a psalm or the pronouncement of thanksgivings and blessings in connection with the Shema, that great word from the sixth chapter of Deuteronomy.

> Hear, O Israel: The LORD our God is one LORD; and you shall love the LORD your God with all your heart, and with all your soul, and with all your might. And these words which I command you this day shall be upon your heart; and you shall teach them diligently to your children . . .

This reflection on God's graciousness would be followed by a time of prayer, closing with the congregation's "Amen!" ("Yes, LORD, let it be fulfilled.")

Then the heart of the service: The senior elder, likely a wizened old man, perhaps with trembling hands, would pull back the curtain and open the wooden cupboard or "ark" where the scrolls containing the very words of God were kept. First a scroll from the Pentateuch, or the books of Moses, would be removed and placed upon a lectern on a raised platform in the middle of the room. One of the elders or a visiting rabbi would read from the scroll first of all in Hebrew. Afterwards the passage would be translated into Aramaic, the language generally spoken in the land. The procedure would be repeated with a reading from the Prophets, and then one of the teachers would give an exposition, often followed by questions and discussion. The service would end with the pronouncement of the benediction, if a priest were present, or a closing prayer from one of the elders. They seem to have done all right under the circumstances, considering the fact that they had no overhead projectors or visiting jazz ensembles; entertainment had to take a back seat to actual worship and learning. They focused on the Word of God, the center around which they had come together.

If a visiting rabbi or teacher were present, he would commonly be asked to speak. This is apparently what happened in Nazareth as Jesus was invited to the platform and the elder handed Him the scroll of Isaiah the prophet. Jesus turned to the passage we would find in chapter 61, and as the people listened, this is what He read:

> The Spirit of the Lord is upon me, because he has anointed me to preach good news to the poor. He has sent me to proclaim release to the captives and recovering of sight to the blind, to set at liberty those who are oppressed, to proclaim the acceptable year of the Lord.

It was a well-known passage of Scripture, referring, as everyone knew, to the Lord's promised Messiah. The very word *messiah* meant "the anointed one," and they understood that Isaiah was speaking of one who would be anointed or specially filled with the Spirit of the Lord to accomplish a special mission. Throughout their history, God's Spirit had filled individuals for particular purposes, often with remarkable results. Their greatest king, David, had been anointed by the prophet Samuel when he was only a teenager, and God's Spirit had come mightily upon David from that day forward. The Spirit made David bold and fearless, and ultimately raised him to the highest position in the land. The people knew what it meant to be anointed by God's Spirit for a special purpose.

The passage chosen that day focuses on the nature of the ministry of the anointed one. He was, Isaiah said, "to preach good news to the poor"—the word *poor* is that used in the Beatitudes to refer to the "poor in spirit" whom God desires to bless. This spirit is expressed a little further on in Isaiah 66 where God says, "But this is the man to whom I will look, he that is humble and contrite in spirit, and trembles at my word." Jesus was saying that the Messiah would bring particularly good news to the person who was truly humble and who truly feared the Lord, trembling at His word.

Then Isaiah goes on to talk about releasing the captives. This word refers primarily to those unfortunate souls who have been captured in war and are so often mistreated. The war Jesus referred to was spiritual warfare, where many captives had been taken—the battle for men's souls carried on in high places by the forces of darkness. The Messiah came to release His people from that oppression and slavery.

"Recovering of sight to the blind" refers to much more than the simple restoration of vision to the sightless, which Jesus had already done, a restoration which served only to enable them to witness the events of life leading ultimately to their own death. As it applies to the Messiah, it clearly refers to the way sin blinds us to the truth. In so many ways, our sin blinds us to the realities of God's world. In doing so, it blinds us, among other things, to *possibility*—we think we cannot expect anything more of ourselves; after all, we are such sinners! Sin has blinded us to the potential we have with God's Spirit at work within us. It blinds us ultimately to the true joy and fulfillment which could be ours. The Messiah, Isaiah says, would enable men and women to see through to the heart of things, to witness the crystalline beauty of God's whole creation, both physical and spiritual.

Not only that, but He would "set at liberty those who are oppressed, [and] proclaim the acceptable year of the Lord." I don't know if that phrase means a lot to you, but it meant a great deal to the people of Israel. It was a reference to the Jubilee Year described in Leviticus 25. Not only were God's people to rest and be refreshed every seventh day, but every seventh year they were to take a sabbatical and allow the land to lie fallow while they drew refreshment from the hand of the Lord. That was His plan for them. He wanted to nurture and to feed them. Then, after seven cycles of seven years, or forty-nine years, they were to sound the trumpet on the Day of Atonement and set aside the entire fiftieth year to "proclaim liberty throughout the land to all its inhabitants." Moses had explained, "It shall be a jubilee for you." And in that year they were to release all captives, forgive all debts, return all property to its original owners, allow the land to lie fallow, and ultimately accept the bounty of the Lord.

All Israel knew this as the ultimate celebration. Their heritage called for many feasts and many celebrations, but this was the climax of all their acts of faith—although they had never been able to bring themselves to trust God quite that far. It was a great idea, if it worked; but each wanted to hang onto his own advantage, his own security. They just could not quite bring themselves to release their slaves, or to release their land, or to release their debtors, or to release their source of income, risking everything on the wager that God would actually meet all their needs and more. The Jubilee year was an idea that never worked out in reality in Israel.

At the appropriate time, however, Isaiah said God would send His specially anointed messenger to proclaim this year of bounty and release: this Jubilee, this great celebration. It would involve a greater liberation than even setting free a slave. He would release His people from fear and from guilt, from the pollution and stain of sin, from captivity to Satan, and from the sad results and consequences of our sin. In fact, as Paul points out in Romans 8, this release from slavery when the Messiah comes would mean more than a release from slavery. Listen to these familiar words from Romans 8 and see what is added:

> For all who are led by the Spirit of God are sons of God. For you did not receive the spirit of slavery to fall back into fear, but you have received the spirit of sonship. When we cry, "Abba! Father!" it is the Spirit himself bearing witness with our spirit that we are children of God, and if children, then heirs, heirs of God and fellow heirs with Christ [verses 14-17a].

More than simply releasing a slave to make it on his own—and often he could not and had to return to a life of slavery—in the Lord's Jubilee, He would make that slave His own son and lavish His own fortune upon him. Here was the acceptable year, here was the jubilee, here was the celebration that would be announced by the Messiah.

It was a passage of surpassing power and hope. And now in Luke 4:20, the evangelist wants you to be there and to sense the impact as Jesus said the most astonishing thing. Verbally Luke puts everything into slow motion here, and we watch as "he closed the book, and gave it back to the attendant, and sat down and the eyes of all in the synagogue were fixed on him. And he began to [speak]." And this is what He said to them: "Today this scripture has been fulfilled in your hearing!"

I expect you could have heard a pin drop. They had heard these promises for so long. Was it a metaphor? An ideal? An inaccessible pledge of a golden age to come? Something we could all hope for and that would encourage us in the difficulties of our lives? The words echoed through the old synagogue, rebounding off the limestone walls: "Today this scripture has been fulfilled in your hearing." Do you hear me, people? While you are listening to me—at this very moment—even here before your very eyes, these words from the prophet Isaiah that you have thought about and reflected upon for so long are being fulfilled in your hearing!

As the words began to soak in, the people had to admit that Jesus had been doing many of those things. He had been restoring sight; He had been restoring hearing; He had been restoring mobility; He had been restoring hope. But the implication, too huge and magnificent to comprehend, was that this man standing before them—this, their fellow townsman—was the promised Messiah! And the Day of the Lord for which they had longed for so many generations was being ushered in even as they listened!

In that one, magical moment, it almost seemed as if it could be true! Jesus had spoken with such inner conviction, freshness, authority, and graciousness that the people sat in astonishment and wonder. Could it be? His wisdom certainly was remarkable, surpassing that of the scribes and the Pharisees. His works were almost inconceivable. They knew His reputation; some had seen His miracles. Could it be?

In the silent moments which followed Jesus' remark, that natural pride which resents the elevation of one over another, or any challenge to established authority, crept into the room and sat, mocking, in the corner, a look of contempt on its face. "Wait a minute. I know this man. Who does He think He is, anyway? He grew up here—went to school with my kids. I had Him make a workbench for me over in His father's shop. How can He make such an outlandish claim?"

He was too familiar, you see. Familiarity does breed contempt. Despite all the wonderful, supportive evidence, their sinful nature was quite capable of suppressing their own excitement in that moment and obscuring the miracle in their midst. It was asking too much. They would not believe it, no matter what evidence was presented.

You and I often feel we have been shortchanged. If only we had been there and could have seen Jesus performing those miracles, it would be easier to believe! Well, these people were there. They saw them—but their eyes were blinded. God's Spirit needs to open blind eyes if we are really to see what lies behind the familiar.

We might stand in judgment over these skeptics, but I think this passage, perhaps more than any other in all of Scripture, speaks to churches full of good people—to churches who are quite certain that perhaps they have already arrived; who have already seen it all; who have had all the familiar explanations and traditions drilled into them from time immemorial; who have the Christian faith neatly bound and packaged (everything fits, you know, and is packed away for safekeeping); who know all the answers before the questions are asked; who are certain nothing new could invade their comfortable interpretation of life and faith to shake things up; who have, in effect, surgically removed the beating heart from the gospel, leaving the corpse intact but certain that it could not get up and do something unexpected, something which might surprise or frighten or embarrass them. Faith is carefully circumscribed in a book for these people. It must never get up off the page and start walking about.

But that is precisely what was happening in the synagogue in Nazareth that day. The Word of God had gotten up off the page and begun to walk about. And if it does that, who knows what it might do next? It just might (in fact, it probably will!) upset the status quo. If the oppressed are actually being liberated, how can we ever be sure that Gentiles, slaves, and women will ever know their place again?

It was just too much. So they blurted out, "We know this man. This is Joseph's son. Where does He get all His unorthodox ideas?" A lot of other folks might be ecstatic about what they had discovered, but those who thought they knew it all quickly determined to let the wind out of His sails.

Jesus was not surprised. "No prophet is acceptable in his own country," He said. It would not be the first time that God had bypassed those who should have known better, those who had His Word but did not expect it to come to life. It had happened with Elijah and Elisha; it has happened throughout history: God has bypassed the people who should have known and gone instead to the people who saw it new and fresh for the first time.

How easy it would be for us to overlook the wonderful things which God's Spirit is doing and intends to do in our midst! We know how God does things. We know what He will do. We do not expect Him to step out of the familiar bounds and do something radical. And we know His people; they're nothing special. Isn't this Joseph's son? Or, [heaven forbid] isn't this Mary's daughter? How in the world could God work through her? We know precisely what God has in mind. We know precisely how God will work. We know precisely how to interpret everything He has ever said. We don't see His Spirit breaking through and doing something extraordinary!

Of course we don't. For our certainty that we have everything figured out is what blinds us. Great things will not happen if we are blind to the reality and the power behind God's Word.

> For this people's heart has grown dull, and their ears are heavy of hearing, and their eyes they have closed, lest they should perceive with their eyes, and hear with their ears, and understand with their heart, and turn for me to heal them (Matthew 13:15).

Each one of us has areas in which we are blind. We are sure we know the answers, but there is a distinct possibility that if we allow God's Word to do it, He might break through and reveal something new to us—something radical which He intends to do. We have to make a choice, whether we will listen with genuinely open hearts, or whether we will circumscribe God with our own expectations.

The people of Nazareth made their choice. They might have let Jesus open their eyes, but they were too defensive, too proud, too insecure to have their world shaken the way the gospel will (I guarantee it) always shake it. They decided to remove the threat. No one was going to be allowed to challenge their answers or their ways of doing things! They had things locked up on purpose, and they didn't want anyone setting loose anything they had under control.

"Filled with wrath," our text tells us, "they rose up and put him out of the city, and led him to the brow of the hill on which their city was built, [intending to] throw him down headlong."

Of course, they could not stop Him altogether. They could only assure themselves that He would go somewhere else to perform His miracles and wonders, that He would go somewhere else to restore the sight of the blind, that He would go somewhere else to release the captives. They could not stop Jesus from setting the world free. They could only decide for themselves whether they would remain confined in the dungeon of their own limited vision. He might have set them free . . . "but passing through the midst of them he went away."

That would be a terrible epitaph. To think that Christ was here, but we were so blind and so resistant that "passing through the midst of them he went away."

Will that be your epitaph as well? Or will you allow yourself to be surprised by the Living God?

Fishermen, Tax Collectors, and Other Sinners

(Luke 5:1-11, 27-32)

It was a grand day, with the sun reflecting off the sparkling blue waters of the lake of Gennesaret, the gem of Galilee, with its sapphire surface nestled in a setting of rich, green hills. The name Gennesaret actually means "garden of abundance," which is precisely what Josephus, a historian and contemporary of Jesus, describes. The area was, he said, "an immense garden of incomparable fertility," rife with luscious date palms, oranges, figs, pomegranates, olives, almonds, and all kinds of nuts, balsam and cypress, vines and castor oil trees.

If you were to visit today, you would find the northwestern shore of the Sea of Galilee to be quiet and pastoral. A low, empty plain reaches back from the shore about two miles toward the mountains which recede into the distance. But in Jesus' day, this narrow coastal plain was one of the most densely populated areas in all of Palestine. Thousands of people lived in a string of perhaps a dozen thriving cities along this coastal plain, harvesting the abundant fruit which grew inland as well as the profusion of fish with which the warm, clear waters of the Sea of Galilee teemed.

On this particular morning one of those fishermen, a big, burly, energetic man named Simon, was working diligently along the shore where he and his partners had stretched their nets over several of the black basalt boulders which lined the water's edge. Simon, I suppose, was quite unaware of the quaint beauty of the nearby village of Capernaum, or of the low, wooded hills behind them, or of the impressive, snow-covered summit of Mount Hermon to the north. He was tired from fishing all night, yet he still had work to do, cleaning the nets; besides, this was all very familiar to him. He had been born in Bethsaida, just a few miles to the east, beyond the Jordan's inlet to the lake.

But when that sleepy little fishing village was rebuilt by Herod's son and dedicated to the Roman Caesar, it had taken on a distinctively pagan culture, and Simon and his brother Andrew had moved to Capernaum where they became partners in a fishing business owned by a man named Zebedee. Along with his two sons, James and John, they had committed their lives to the trade of supplying fish for the population. In fact, Zebedee, being a rather wealthy and industrious man, marketed his product extensively in Jerusalem and had many business contacts there.

Tired and preoccupied as he was, however, Simon was distracted by the drama which was unfolding around him that morning. A great crowd of people had gathered and seemed to be growing with each passing minute. Periodically, I imagine, Peter cursed and waved back some overzealous spectator scrambling over the rocks and threatening to tangle his nets. The object of all this attention was Jesus, a man Simon had met a year earlier when his brother Andrew had brought him excitedly to the shores of the Jordan River to introduce them. Andrew was convinced Jesus was the Messiah. Simon was uncertain, but he had been impressed with this lean and sunburned man who had apparently just returned from some powerful experience in the desert. There was something about Him that appealed to Simon, and they had certainly made a connection. In fact, Jesus had given him a nickname, Peter (or "Cephas" in the Aramaic), meaning "rock." Simon Peter was uncertain why, but he was flattered by the personal attention, and in any case the name had stuck.

In fact, since that spring of 28 A.D. had been a sabbatical year, with its consequent disruption of the normal business cycles, Zebedee had given the young men some time off. So he and Andrew, his brother, along with James and John, had traveled a bit with Jesus. People had begun to proclaim Him a prophet, and Peter had to admit he had seen Him do some remarkable things.

He had been with Him at a wedding in Cana when He turned several great pitchers of water into wine; since then, Peter had seen Him heal a number of people, including Peter's own mother-in-law. The remarkable thing was that He did it with such natural and irresistible authority. He simply spoke, or touched, and people were healed or demons were cast out.

The men had eventually needed to get back to their fishing business, but continued to hear reports of Jesus' growing reputation. Over in Nazareth, Jesus had been thrown out of the synagogue for teachings which seemed to border on blasphemy. But nearly everywhere, the common people spoke of Him with awe and respect.

Now He had recently shown up in Capernaum, where He had taken the population by storm. Everywhere you went, people were talking about His wonderful miracles and astonishing authority. This morning He had come down to the waterfront, and now the crowd was practically pushing Him into the lake as they jostled one another in an attempt to see and hear Him. Working in the crowded space along the shore, Simon Peter listened to Jesus talk about the kingdom of God as if it were a place with which He was intimately familiar. It would be great, he thought, if you had time to contemplate such things, but a man had to earn a living. Besides, Peter admitted, if he had anything to do with who got into such a kingdom, he certainly wouldn't let a calloused old sinner like himself inside! He tried to live right, of course, and having family responsibilities had mellowed him a bit, but the people he worked with were tough; if you backed away, someone was always there to take advantage of you. If Jesus really knew what he was like in his heart of hearts, Peter doubted He would have invited him to accompany Him on His travels the year earlier.

"Simon." Peter looked up, surprised to hear his name on the lips of this famous man. Jesus had climbed into Simon and Andrew's boat. The crowd had made it impossible for Him to stand on the shore any longer. "Would you push out a bit from the shore?" Jesus asked. Peter scrambled down into the water to the side of the boat. Uncoiling several loops of rope from the stone anchor, he pushed the wooden boat out several yards into the shallow water. Jesus sat down and continued teaching the people from the boat.

When He had finished speaking, He called to Simon once again, "Put out into deep water, and let down the nets for a catch." Peter was surprised. This was not the best time of the day for fishing, and besides, they had already been out all night and had just gotten everything cleaned up. "Master, we've worked hard all night and haven't caught anything," Peter could not resist saying. "But because you say so, I will let down the nets."

Peter signaled his brother Andrew and a couple of the hired helpers, and they loaded the nets back into the boat, pulled up the anchor, and began to row back out through the crowded harbor toward the deep water. Once clear of the other boats, the helpers yanked at the knots, unfurling the sail which dropped from the yardarms. When they had secured the inverted triangle at the base, the sail filled with the warm, offshore breeze, driving the boat forward as the prow cut easily through the waves. A relatively short distance from the shore, Jesus instructed them to furl the sail once more and let down the nets. They did, although no doubt skeptically, for they must have wondered how a carpenter could know more about fishing than they did. But immediately their purse seine enclosed a great shoal of fish—so large, we are told, that the net began to break. Signaling frantically to James and John, their partners who were watching from the shore, Peter and his shipmates struggled until the two boats, now loaded to the gunwales and already beginning to ship water, finally made it back to land.

On shore everyone was in a great deal of commotion, transferring the fish to the barrels in which they would be hauled to the market or processed, and exclaiming about the astonishing catch. Peter, however, usually at the center of every activity, stood apart from the turmoil. What was happening with the fish no longer interested him. His eyes were fixed on Jesus, who stood quietly to one side, searching the faces of the excited fishermen.

Suddenly Peter knew that those eyes which could see a shoal of fish concealed in the dark depths of a lake could also see the accumulation of sins concealed in the dark depths of his soul. He found himself reviewing all the coarse, insensitive words he had ever spoken. He remembered the shameful conversations he had often had with the rough crowd who bought his fish. He thought about how many times he had stretched the truth to extend his profit margin. Wincing with the pain of it all, he thought how thoughtless and selfish he had often been with his wife, and how many ugly and degrading thoughts he had harbored in his mind. He began to remember dark, troubling sins long forgotten . . . and now, with an overwhelming sense of his own guilt and failure, he knew that he did not want those eyes turned upon him. We, all of us, can hold our heads up in public only because no one really knows what goes on in the depths of our hearts. With a sense of shame approaching panic, Peter fell at Jesus' feet crying, "Depart from me, O Lord, for I am a sinful man!"

Instead, Jesus looked into Peter's eyes. And although you could see that His gaze did indeed plumb the depths of Peter's soul, yet there was great compassion in those eyes, and not a trace of condemnation. Jesus could see Peter's grief over his sins and knew the fear and the pain welling up in Peter's troubled soul meant that he was just the sort of person He was looking for. So He said to him gently, "Don't be afraid, from now on you will catch men." There was such a look of confidence and grace in Jesus' eyes that Peter was vanquished. If this man could look into his polluted soul and still love him, Peter knew that he could not be any place other than with Him.

All his life Peter had managed to live with himself by refusing to face who he really was. But here was a man who did know who he was. Here was a man who saw every slimy little sin swimming around in the dark ocean of his soul, and who could somehow deal with that and not only love him the way we might love some poor, pitiful creature who can't help himself, but love him in a way that showed He believed Peter was a valuable person who could do something grandly worthwhile. It was more than Peter could ever have dreamed. He knew he would follow this man anywhere.

Jesus had challenged these men before. They had had time to reflect upon it. And now, one by one, Andrew and James and John also came to Him. "You asked us before if we would follow you," they said. "If you will have us, we will go with you anywhere." They had had a year to watch Jesus—sometimes up close, sometimes at a distance. They had been challenged to follow Him. But not until they realized how utterly lost they would be without

Him, were they ready to leave everything behind to become His disciples.

And that is what they did. They pulled their boats on shore and walked away. Zebedee and his hired helpers would have to go elsewhere for the manpower needed to continue the fishing business. These men knew they had to follow Jesus.

The story would be repeated several more times during the next few weeks as Jesus selected a group of twelve unlikely men to accompany Him from village to village, observing the hand of God at work, hearing the message of the Kingdom and seeing it applied to the lives of women and men in each of those communities. These twelve would form the core of His followers, but many others would be called as well, including some influential women who would respond to His call and participate in His ministry in a variety of ways. Three women—Mary from Magdala, Joanna, and Susanna—actually accompanied Him during one of His preaching tours through Galilee, something unheard of in that day. Jesus was collecting a group of people who would be His disciples.

A few days after calling the four young fishermen, Jesus astounded them all by calling a hated tax collector by the name of Levi (or Matthew) into His circle. Levi was one of the most despised men in Capernaum and the disciples knew him well—too well, I think Peter would have complained. Every time he arrived at shore with his catch of fish, Levi was there to skim the revenue for the Roman government. Capernaum was a border town and Levi worked at the customs office, collecting the tax for the Roman occupational government on all goods transferred. He was considered a traitor by his countrymen; first, because he served the pagan Roman government, and second, because he made a very good living off their produce. Most were sure they had never known an honest tax collector. Bribes and extortion were commonplace. They could say nothing good about such a parasite.

But Levi was an intelligent and observant man, well versed in the Hebrew Scriptures and quite aware of the stir which Jesus was causing in his community. Perhaps he was at the synagogue when Jesus cast out demons; no doubt he watched as the streets filled with people at sundown on the Sabbath and Jesus worked late into the night, healing all who came. Later, this former tax collector would write that it seemed to him the prophecy concerning the "Suffering Servant" was being fulfilled where Isaiah wrote, "He took up our infirmities and carried our diseases." Matthew had watched Jesus, and knowing the Scriptures as he did, he had begun to wonder if this remarkable man might not be specially anointed by God.

On the day Matthew's life was to change, however, he was busy with his books and the supervision of his assistants as they counted the flocks of sheep and goats and weighed the barrels of fish and produce. As people came and went, Matthew hardly looked up from his work. He had become immune to the complaints and curses of his countrymen. He had a job to do, that was all; if they didn't like it, well, that was their problem. But sometime during the day, in the midst of all the confusion, Matthew became aware that someone had just called his name, and that the tone was far different from anything he normally heard. Looking up, he found himself staring into the eyes of that very man, Jesus.

Up to that moment, Matthew had probably been quite certain that he could remain anonymous. He was a quiet man. He is the only man among the disciples who is never quoted as having said anything. The New Testament opens with his written account of the life of Jesus, but I think we would have found Matthew to be the one man in a crowd to keep his mouth shut and his eyes open. There was a certain protection in his reticence. He could observe all the activity from the safe haven of his customs post and not get involved. Perhaps he could justify his dishonesty and his contempt for the people as part of a job he had to do. But at this moment, all his excuses dissolved, and before this wonderful man who gave Himself so unreservedly for others, Matthew knew he had spent his entire life serving himself. Indeed, he had spent his entire life deceiving himself.

"Follow me," Jesus was saying—saying to him, to Matthew, the person everyone else wanted to send away. Jesus was saying, "Come and be my disciple." Something in Jesus' eyes told him he could put all his misspent life behind him, that although the price might seem great, the compensation would be greater still.

Matthew took one last look around the customs house. He smiled to himself as he thought how little of what he really wanted in life could ever be found there. Patting his chief assistant on the back, he told him he was leaving and that he wouldn't be back. The man looked stunned, and stood looking after him as Matthew stepped out of the toll house and walked up to Jesus. Jesus was looking at him as if to say, "I knew it. I knew you had it in you. I knew you were more than a tax collector at heart. You won't regret this decision."

That night, the rest of the disciples made their way uncomfortably to the wealthy suburb where Matthew had his home. He had invited them to a great feast and had invited many of his friends and colleagues as well. The disciples no doubt were self-conscious about their appearance and quite unsure how to conduct themselves in this stratum of society. The large, luxurious rooms with silk hangings and brocaded furniture were quite unlike the simple fare most common laborers enjoyed. And the company included many of Matthew's wealthy colleagues and neighbors, very sophisticated and very pagan. It was not a society at all familiar to the disciples.

Jesus, however, seemed perfectly at ease accepting Matthew's lavish hospitality. Throughout the evening He engaged his friends in animated, challenging conversation. They listened to Him talk openly and sincerely about the love of God for them and the possibility of new beginnings for those who would turn from their sin to follow Him. They had to admit they were sinners. Yet their hearts were drawn to this man. They could see the compelling attraction of His transparent witness and they knew why their friend Matthew had announced he was giving up his position and would be selling all he had to go and support the ministry of this man Jesus.

Before the evening was over, some of the disciples slipped out early, probably to escape their own discomfort in the presence of these irreligious folks. What do you say to a pagan? Once outside, however, the disciples encountered some scribes and Pharisees, who immediately began to challenge them about eating and drinking with tax collectors and sinners. The disciples did not know what to say. For all we know, they were probably inclined to agree. But as they stood there in the darkness, trying to think of a defense for their Master, Jesus stepped out from the house and approached with an irrefutable answer. "Those who are well have no need of a physician," He said, "but those who are sick; I have not come to call the righteous, but sinners to repentance."

It was not, of course, that Jesus had nothing to offer the religious folks. It was just that He knew only those who admitted their souls were diseased would ever look to Him for a cure.

What was it that qualified someone to be Jesus' disciple? He did not call the great or those who were particularly religious. He did not call the most highly educated or the best teachers or even those with the greatest faith. He didn't call the beautiful people, the powerful people. Just two things seemed to characterize the disciples Jesus called: a certain honesty about themselves, a willingness to see themselves as sinners; and an equal willingness to be made whole and new by the Master.

Those two things alone characterize the people Jesus called to be His disciples. I don't see anything else to distinguish this undistinguished group which ultimately turned the world upside-down. They were honest about themselves, and they were willing to be made new. That's all.

Do you know that the same criteria apply to those whom Jesus calls to be His most effective disciples today? Like Peter and Matthew, we must be willing to see ourselves for who we really are. If we think we are Somebody, and the church and the kingdom ought to be grateful we are around, chances are we really don't have much Jesus can use.

On the other hand, we cannot simply wallow in our sinfulness. We must be willing to be transformed, and even to pay a great price for that transformation. But knowing what the compensation is, Peter and Matthew were not afraid to do just that. For discipleship is for sinners—sinners who are willing to be made new.

An Astonishing Authority

(Mark 1:21-28)

Above everything else, Jesus was a teacher. "You shall know the truth," He had said, "and the truth shall make you free." It was the great desire of Jesus' heart that people would come to know what was true, the only thing that would transform their lives and set them free. The world had lost its way, and Jesus knew that His business was to help them find "the way," the way back to Him who had created them for a purpose.

He taught people how to live in relationship to each other and to God—two critical skills almost totally lost by our society. It all fit together within the larger theme of the "kingdom of God," the heart of His teaching. The way into the kingdom of God, He said, was through repentance, trust, and obedience. We were to turn from our own way to follow Him. That was the content of Jesus' teaching: the kingdom of God, finding our way back to God, following Him, and obeying Him.

More than fifty times in the Gospels, Jesus is referred to as "teacher." Other titles also were significant: "Messiah" and "Son of God," among the most important. But the predominant title by which He was addressed during His earthly life was "teacher." That is how people saw Him; that is how people related to Him. And indeed, He was a remarkable teacher. Everywhere he went, it seemed He was always explaining the real significance of things.

What a tremendous privilege it must have been to walk with Him and to hear His commentary on life!

His style was different from anything the people had seen. For one thing, it was extemporaneous. Their teachers always had long, formal recitations on prescribed themes. But Jesus gave a spontaneous, living commentary on life and its meaning—vivid and powerful, packed with stark, memorable images and phrases such as, "Blessed are the poor in spirit, for theirs is the kingdom of heaven" or "You are the salt of the earth . . . you are the light of the world." It was Jesus who said, "It is easier for a camel to go through the eye of a needle than for a rich man to enter heaven"; it was He who said, "the gate is narrow and the way is hard that leads to life, and those who find it are few." Jesus said things in a way that you just couldn't forget. He was an outstanding teacher.

While He said things in a new way, however, *what* He had to say itself was far from new or unorthodox. Always it was deeply rooted in the Old Testament Scriptures which the people had known all their lives. He simply gave new insight into familiar themes. He constantly illustrated His teachings with everyday experiences: plucking off a head of grain as He walked through a field and using it to explain how the kingdom of God grows; noticing a flock of birds flying up as they walked along the way and using them to illustrate God's personal care and attention for each member of His creation.

Always His teaching was immediately relevant to the people's daily lives, something which could not always be said about the teaching of the scribes. Always His teaching was powerfully engaging, for it came so clearly from a genuine love and concern for those who listened.

What stood out about Jesus' teaching above anything else, however, was His authority—an authority at once captivating for those who heard it and alarming to those challenged by it. Mark, a close friend and associate of Peter, stresses this point. "When the Sabbath came, Jesus went into the synagogue and began to teach." This was not unusual, of course. There were itinerant preachers in the land and when they would arrive at a synagogue, they would be invited to read the Scripture and comment upon it. But now listen to the difference. Mark writes,

The people were amazed [many versions use the stronger word *astonished*] at his teaching, because he taught them as one who had authority, not as the teachers of the law.

Jesus taught with an authority that permitted neither debate nor even theoretical reflection. Consistently He confronted His hearers with the absolute claim of God on their lives. His teachings were not open to discussion or negotiation. He said with absolute authority, "this is what God requires," period—or maybe exclamation point! There was no debate.

Jesus challenged our natural insubordination with a captivating and unapologetic authority so powerful and compelling that it unsettled people. The word translated *amazed* or *astonished* or *unsettling* quite literally means "blown away." It means to strike one out of his wits. His authority was so striking that people were dumbfounded when they encountered it. It was unlike anything they had ever experienced, and they knew instinctively that they could ignore it only at their peril.

The source of Jesus' authority was that He spoke as the very Founder of the universe. The Gospel of John explains that Jesus was with God the Father "in the beginning," and that "all things were made through him." He holds the whole universe together through the power of His Word. He had come into the world as the agent of the Father's will, to redeem that world and bring it back into harmony with God. "My teaching," Jesus had explained to those who challenged it, "comes from him who sent me. If any one chooses to do God's will, he will find out whether my teaching comes from God or whether I speak on my own."

Now you understand what an incredible treasure is contained in the words of Jesus if He speaks for the One who made the universe! Without a word from God, we are left to guess about the most important things in the world. But if we have access here to the very mind of God, then every question of significance can be addressed: Where did we come from? What is the purpose of our living? To what end should we dedicate our lives? How can we know right from wrong? If Jesus' authority is established, the lights come on in the universe!

One Sabbath, Jesus came to Capernaum, that thriving fishing village on the northwest coast of the Sea of Galilee, and entered the synagogue with all the others. Attendance at the synagogue was required, though undoubtedly many found it disappointing. This particular morning, Jesus' presence had stirred a great deal of excitement. He had already performed many miracles throughout the area, and many were proclaiming Him a prophet in the spirit of the great Elijah. So they came to the synagogue that morning with great anticipation, hoping to hear more of the electrifying Word of God which seemed to come so consistently from His lips.

And they were not disappointed. While the people were not allowed to exclaim aloud or interrupt a synagogue address, there was nonetheless a great stirring among the crowd as the people listened to Jesus. No one had ever spoken to them with such compelling authority.

Somewhere along the line—about midway through the sermon and so unexpectedly that at first the people were confused as to what was taking place—a high-pitched voice rang out from the congregation, "What do you want with us, Jesus of Nazareth? Have you come to destroy us?" You can imagine the reaction to such a cry from the congregation on a Sunday morning! It was a cry both of defiance and of terror, and scalps throughout the crowd tingled at the piercing, otherworldly tone of the voice. A man was standing in the middle of the synagogue, his eyes wild with excitement, his fists raised in defiance.

The people had seen such behavior before; they knew the man was possessed by an evil spirit. He never should have been allowed into this place! Perhaps the rabbi and some of the elders would remove him before he created any further disturbance.

Literally, the man's challenge was, "What have we to do with you?" That phrase was used in the Old Testament when one king or army would challenge another. It was used often in the context of combat or judgment. In effect he was saying, "You have no business with us—not yet." Speaking in the plural, the man apparently spoke for all the demonic powers. Jesus had invaded their territory and the demon recognized it as a mortal threat. "I know what you are about," he was saying, "you have come to destroy us." He was aware of a battle going on that the people in the congregation had missed entirely.

And then, as the congregation buzzed with response, the man cried out, "I know who you are—the Holy One of God!" The rest of the people did not know that, at least not yet. But this demon, possessed of a spiritual knowledge to which the people were not privy, recognized Jesus as a mortal enemy. While the sick who came to Jesus for healing consistently called him "Lord" or "Teacher," "Son of David," "Master," or some such term, the demoniacs addressed him as "the Holy One of God," "the Son of God," or "the Son of the Most High God." They were aware of who He was long before the people became aware.

The phenomenon was so prevalent that some time later, James, Jesus' brother, would challenge the Jews concerning the nature of belief. He would say to them in that familiar verse from James, "You believe that there is one God. Good! Even the demons believe that—and shudder."

Here this demon, speaking through the mouth of the one possessed, challenged Jesus on His purpose for being there and identified Him as the Holy One of God. Suddenly Jesus stopped preaching and fixed the man in His gaze. Sternly He said, "Be quiet! Come out of him!" and the man began to shake violently. Luke, in his account, says the demon threw him down in front of all the people, and then with a ghastly and appalling shriek, the demon fled from him. And the people were amazed.

It's quite possible the people may not have been amazed for the same reason you and I would be amazed. We would be amazed to see such an event because most likely none of us has ever seen anything like it. One of the great ironies of our reading of the New Testament is the way we pass over the stories of Jesus' casting out demons, as if He were shooing away a stray dog.

Because we don't encounter this sort of thing very often, we have a tendency to dismiss it as a primitive phenomenon, or to consider it no more than an unsophisticated description of a disease like epilepsy. But these incidents are central to understanding what Jesus was about. If you read through the Gospels with an ear to listen to how many times Jesus confronted the spirits of evil, you will recognize two worlds were colliding in a battle to the death between the forces of evil and the forces of good.

M. Scott Peck, a medical doctor and psychologist who at the time had no faith other than a vague identification with Buddhist and Islamic mysticism, witnessed such an encounter between the forces of good and evil. These battles are yet taking place, whether you and I see it and are aware of it or not. Listen to Dr. Peck as he describes, as a scientist and an objective observer, what he witnessed. In his book, *The People of the Lie*, he describes two exorcisms which even he had to admit were face-to-face encounters with the spiritual forces of wickedness. In one, as the demonic finally surfaced and spoke to the team working to exorcise it, he watched the patient's face transformed by what he calls "an incredibly contemptuous grin of utter hostile malevolence." He said he felt he had come face-to-face with Satan. If that was bad, the other surfaced in an even more hideous form:

> The patient suddenly resembled a writhing snake of great strength, viciously attempting to bite the team members. More frightening than the writhing body, however, was the face. The eyes were hooded with lazy reptilian torpor— except when the reptile darted out in attack, at which moment the eyes would open wide with blazing hatred.[1]

Peck concludes,

> Despite these frequent darting moments, what upset me the most was the extraordinary sense of a fifty-million-year-old heaviness I received from this serpentine being. It caused me to despair of the success of the exorcism.[2]

The entire team felt it was in the presence of "something absolutely alien and inhuman."

This is a firsthand experience from a contemporary professional, a man who is still living and writing. What he saw was similar to what the people of Capernaum in the synagogue witnessed that day. But not identical! The difference lies in the extraordinary amount of effort and prayer required in the modern incident. As Dr. Peck describes it, "the first (and easier) [exorcism] required a team of seven highly trained professionals to work four days, twelve to sixteen hours a day." He talks about how important it was that the team outnumber the demons, and that they recognize the reality of the risk to them. The second involved a team of nine men and women, who worked twelve to twenty hours a day for three days. In each case, the patient had to be physically restrained, one for almost an entire day. When it came down to the actual expulsion of the demon, it required what Peck describes as "the desperate prayers of the team . . . for God or Christ to come to the rescue." And they experienced precisely that.

In stark contrast to such a massive and exhaustive effort, Jesus simply looked at this man and said, "Be quiet! Come out of him!" And he did! Is it any wonder that these people, far more familiar than we with the spiritual forces of evil, looked at one another in astonishment and said, "What is this? A new teaching—and with authority! He even gives orders to evil spirits and they obey him." There was not a moment's resistance. No resistance could be garnered to offset the authority of Jesus.

Whatever else we may say about Jesus' teaching, this is central. Unlike any other teacher before or since, He spoke with an irresistible authority. It was the authority Isaiah had seen centuries before:

So shall my word be that goes forth from my mouth; it shall not return to me empty, but it shall accomplish that which I purpose, and prosper in the thing for which I sent it (Isaiah 55:11).

Anyone with a rebellious spirit has to find it a frightening thing to encounter such an irresistible word—a word which you know is not making a suggestion or offering advice, a word which brooks no argument, no protest, but a word which can and ultimately will achieve its intention. There is something pitiful about that demon shrieking out Jesus' true name and hatefully announcing its own destruction at His hands, yet without remorse. I suspect such a scene will not be uncommon on the day of the Lord's judgment.

Jesus is utterly authoritative; He is able to accomplish what He speaks. I cannot stress enough that God's Word is not simply good advice. Never think that the New and Old Testaments are simply good advice, something useful if you could muster up enough strength and motivation to do what they say. God's Word is real and living and it will compel conformity. Either we will conform to that Word and live, or we will continue to resist that Word and die.

The situation was really that stark in the confrontation between good and evil that day in the synagogue in Capernaum. And if it was true there, it is true here. Our eyes, perhaps, have not seen the reality of the spiritual world as vividly as Mark describes it. But the fact is we do not wrestle against flesh and blood, but against spiritual hosts of wickedness in high places.

Yet we serve a God whose Word is a living word, and if we will align ourselves with that Word, we will find in it the strength to resist even the most discouraging of the elements that we might be called upon to face. Victory ultimately is on the side of Him who created, who sustains, and who will bring His world to that grand climax which He has promised. The question for you and for me is whether we will conform to His Word and live, or whether we will resist that Word and be broken by it.

Notes

1. M. Scott Peck, *The People of the Lie* (New York: Simon and Schuster, 1983), 196.

2. Ibid.

That's Incredible!

(Luke 7:1-23)

If people were astonished by Jesus' authority, they were incredulous about His miracles. Immediately after He delivered His incomparable Sermon on the Mount, Jesus entered Capernaum and received anquished word of a centurion's servant who was ill and near death.

Now, skeptics might say that these primitive people had no way of knowing whether the man was in fact on the verge of death. They might allege that reports of miracles are simply unsophisticated attempts to explain what we do not understand, and that the servant's "miraculous" recovery was nothing more than a coincidence. But I would caution against underestimating the knowledge of what some consider to be "primitive people."

How many people have you seen die? Most of us are protected from witnessing death firsthand. The average adolescent in that society had seen more people die than most of us will see in a lifetime. These people were not ignorant about death. They were not ignorant about the laws of nature and, therefore, quick to attribute natural events to the supernatural. In fact, quite the opposite was true. Joseph, for example, knew as well as the modern gynecologist where babies come from. That is why he recognized the virgin birth as a miracle; it did not follow the normal pattern. What happened was not what one would have expected to happen according to the laws of nature.

So here it was quite evident to them that the centurion's servant really was about to die. Likely he had lost consciousness, perhaps he was having difficulty breathing and could no longer ingest food or water, nor eliminate the toxins which were poisoning his body. They had seen it many times before. They knew what was happening.

In any event, the centurion, who was a good man with a healthy respect for the Jewish faith, had heard the stories of Jesus' miracles. He hoped that, since Jesus was in the area, He could be persuaded to try to heal his highly valued servant. Luke tells us it was actually some of the elders of the synagogue who came to Jesus with the request, so it may be that the centurion only longed for such a solution, but would not himself have asked for the miracle.

As Jesus approached, the centurion sent word that the Master need not actually come into his home. It wasn't that he lacked hospitality, but rather that he knew the laws of the Jews. He knew that for Jesus to come into the home of a Gentile would ritually defile him. Therefore he told Jesus that if He would only give the command, his servant would be healed. He explained that he himself stood in a chain of command which gave him the authority to direct other men, implying that he understood that Jesus' authority flowed from the power that creates and sustains life itself—otherwise, His order to heal would not be followed. Impressed by this man's great insight into the nature of His authority, Jesus gives the command and the centurion's servant is healed immediately.

But if this miracle suggests Jesus' authority to command life itself, what He did next was absolutely mind boggling. Approaching the city of Nain to the southwest of Capernaum some days later, Jesus met a large crowd of mourners carrying a bier on which lay the body of a young man who had recently died. This was a particularly tragic death because the man was the only son of a woman who had also lost her husband. A woman could not work, so the widow's only means of support was gone. She would be reduced to begging or to charity; but at the moment she was feeling the terrible, desolate grief that only a parent who has lost a child can understand.

Jesus was filled with compassion, or as the New International Version translates it, "his heart went out to her" and He said to her, "Don't cry."

Rather than immediately complying with His directive, I imagine the crying intensified as she thought about her loss. In any case, Jesus went on to do something which would give her reason not to cry. He walked over, touched the coffin, and the pallbearers stopped—perhaps in confusion over this highly unusual interruption. Then Jesus said, "Young man, I say to you, get up!"

And then, the very last thing any of them could have imagined actually took place. The young man sat up and he began to talk to them. This was an unimaginable phenomenon, and the Revised Standard Version describes their reaction best: "Fear seized them all." The New International Version says they were "in awe," but I think they were terrified to see what had just taken place—"What kind of power has been unleashed here?"

Somehow they had to place such a remarkable event in perspective, and they rightly glorified God, the Author and Giver of Life, as the source of this miracle. "A great prophet has appeared among us," they said. "God has come to help his people." There could be no other interpretation for what had taken place. The One who gave life must be responsible for this astonishing miracle. And the news that Jesus had done this spread rapidly throughout the surrounding country.

Eventually the news came to John the Baptist, languishing in prison for his testimony to the work of God. Understandably, John had become deeply discouraged about the course of events. He could not be sure that what had begun with such promise in the revival he had nourished was not now disintegrating. So he sent his disciples to ask whether Jesus was the Messiah he had anticipated. "In that [very] hour," the text says, Jesus cured many who had diseases, plagues, and evil spirits. He also restored the sight of many who were blind. Then He turned to John's disciples and said,

Go back and report to John what you have seen and heard: The blind receive sight, the lame walk, those who have leprosy are cured, the deaf hear, the dead are raised, and the good news is preached to the poor.

I would have expected the last item on the list to be the resurrection—people were healed, their sight restored (the miracles just got more and more spectacular), even the dead were raised. But the final item on Jesus' list is that the good news was preached to the poor. "Blessed," He says, "is the man who does not fall away on account of me."

It was a stunning confirmation of the prediction of the prophet Isaiah, who had said of the Lord's anointed, "'Behold, your God . . . will come and save you.'" Then what will happen? How will you know that God has come to be present among you and to bring salvation? "Then the eyes of the blind shall be opened, and the ears of the deaf unstopped; then shall the lame man leap like a hart, and the tongue of the dumb sing for joy."

Those miracles confirmed what Jesus had taught earlier in the synagogue in Nazareth, when He claimed to fulfill the prophecy of the One who, as the Lord's anointed, would bring "good news to the poor," would bring God's salvation, would bring the answer to the judgment that was facing those who had rebelled against God. The evidence of this would be the mighty miracles they would see performed. So the miracles were not only intended to accomplish wonderful things, although they did that; they were also intended to establish Jesus' identity and ultimately to give credibility to the good news He had come to proclaim.

You understand, then, the role of Jesus' miracles. They were a proof of the existence of this Person or Force beyond nature who could act within it. That's good news! They revealed Him as the Power who could reverse the very forces of death and destruction that plague our world. That is certainly good news! And they revealed Jesus as the agent of that great reversal. Talk about good news! Anyone who came to Jesus would find himself or herself in touch with the only Person or Power in the universe who could turn back the awful forces which continually preyed upon the bodies and spirits of the human race. Such a person would be in personal touch with the source from which life itself flows. The One who multiplied the loaves and the fishes was the One who multiplied the grain in the fields and the fish in the sea every day of the year. The source of all that abundant life was with them. The one who reversed the flow of life into decay and death and turned it around so that it flowed back into grand life again was in their midst.

If it were true, it had to be the greatest good news this poor, struggling world could ever encounter. And those astonishing, irrefutable miracles established the credibility of that good news. The climax of that list, the very top thing, was not the acts of healing themselves but the good news that the God who had created them and who chose to redeem them was active in their world to bring about their ultimate salvation.

It is tremendously significant that we see the miracles of Jesus as the proof positive of His person and His intent in our world. When we have done so, we may say with Peter, when asked whether we will follow Him or go our own way, "Lord, to whom shall we go? You have the words of eternal life. We believe and know that you are the Holy One of God."

That, I think, is the ultimate conclusion of this passage of Scripture, but I do want to address one other question with which you may be struggling. The question is: If our Lord is able to perform such good and powerful miracles, why does He not do it all the time? If our Lord is capable of doing such wonderful things, why does He not do it for us regularly? Granting that He has made faith a prerequisite for miracles, nevertheless, it seems to us that He does not always work miracles even if the requisite faith is present. So we are confused. Why will He not protect His own from any accident or injury? Why will He not answer every sincere prayer for healing? Why will He not stay the hand of death from those He loves? Certainly He is capable of doing this. So why does He so often choose not to do so?

The answer to this question is not so difficult as we have often made it. The answer is that our Lord is interested only in the final miracle. All His other miracles prove Him capable of working that final miracle—the final reversal of all death. They prove Him capable of establishing His reign where death and decay and disappointment have no more power and where life erupts with ecstatic joy and exuberance, as it did when Jesus first performed those miracles. We have a foretaste of all these things in His miracles. But while capable of all miracles, He will in His great love and wisdom and compassion, work only those which will bring us to that one miracle which really counts—the miracle of a life transformed and brought into His spectacular kingdom.

I think it likely that frequent miracles would make us all quite careless. If we could be assured that God would always intervene and change the course of nature to our advantage, we would never learn self-discipline and self-control. We would never learn dependence upon Him. We would not even take death seriously enough to prepare for it. God, in His ultimate wisdom and compassion, must ration His miracles, granting just enough to assure us that He is indeed the source of them all, while at the same time keeping us from presuming upon His constant intervention. He intends that we learn to be like Him and walk with Him. Whether we recover from a particular operation or disease is utterly inconsequential in comparison to whether we receive eternal life through casting ourselves upon His care. That is the only miracle in which He is ultimately interested.

In the movie version of Tolstoy's great novel, War and Peace, Prince Andre and the Czar are considering strategy the night before their great battle with the French. As they pore over the maps, the young prince asks, "Will we win the battle tomorrow?" The Czar's answer is immediate and abrupt, "I think not." A look of panic spreads over the young prince's face. "But what if we do lose this battle?" he asks in great alarm. "What will become of us?"

The aging monarch looks at the young prince with compassion and understanding. "We don't count the battles," he says. "We only count the last battle. The last battle is the only one that really matters."[1]

That same wisdom applies to miracles as well. It is only the final miracle that really matters. It is not my day-to-day healing that matters, but the final miracle of my resurrection with Christ.

Will I participate in that final miracle that God has prepared for those who know Him and love Him and have come to trust Him? All our experiences of pain and suffering and fear and confusion and discontent, all of those experiences from which we would love to be freed, prepare us to accept Christ's ultimate solution. Should He relieve those circumstances in advance, it is likely that we would never give ourselves wholly to Him—the singular act which assures us of participation in that final miracle.

Still, understand that He has not really withheld anything from us at all. In giving us that final miracle, He gives us all the other miracles. Once that final miracle is ours, all other miracles are ours as well. All of them: the abundance of life, the reversal of death and decay, the power of the Spirit to act within the natural world. All of those things we shall enjoy for an eternity in His presence. It is not the individual miracles we are concerned about; we can sacrifice those to receive the final miracle—the everlasting life promised those who place their trust in the Miracle Worker, the man who has the powers of all creation at His disposal.

Note

1. Retold by Robert L. Wise, *When There Is No Miracle* (Glendale, CA: Regal Books, 1977), 48.

A Time to Celebrate

(Luke 19:28-40)

Algernon Charles Swinburne was a nineteenth-century English poet and critic whose work is noted for its vitality and for the music of its language. As a young man in his late twenties, he published a volume of poems and ballads renowned both for their sensuality and their fiercely anti-Christian sentiments. The Christianity which he saw in his day was so totally at odds with his own exuberant celebration of life that he could not help but lash out at the Founder of our faith with this memorable line: "Thou hast conquered, O pale Galilean; and the world has grown gray with thy breath!"

Whether the church deserved this censure or not, certainly Jesus did not deserve it. Remember the ringing words of the angel announcing his birth?

> Behold, I bring you good tidings of great joy, which shall be to all people; for unto you is born this day in the city of David a Savior which is Christ the Lord.

The celebration had begun! Even the site of Jesus' first miracle highlighted this. It was not performed on some great spiritual occasion, but at a wedding feast in Cana of Galilee where (sometimes to our embarrassment) He turned the water into wine—a drink the psalmist says God had given "to gladden the heart of men."

Swinburne's charge against Jesus is not altogether dissimilar from Jesus' own charge against the religious establishment of His day. He thought the world had grown gray from the breath of the Pharisees—those traditional churchmen we have unfortunately chosen as our role models, even as we criticize them. Jesus asked,

> But to what shall I compare this generation? It is like children sitting in the market places and calling to their playmates, "We piped to you, and you did not dance; we wailed, and you did not mourn." For John came neither eating nor drinking, and they say, "He has a demon;" the Son of man came eating and drinking, and they say, "Behold, a glutton and a drunkard, a friend of tax collectors and sinners!" (Matthew 11:16-19).

People who really knew Jesus, of course, could not help but celebrate. It came down to that. Even John the Baptist's disciples could not figure this out, since all the religious people they knew were very solemn; they did things appropriately and in order. When questioned about this, Jesus answered simply, "Can the wedding guests mourn as long as the bridegroom is with them?" As the writer of the Old Testament book of Ecclesiastes had said, "[There is] a time to mourn, [but also] a time to dance." And, as Jesus' disciples figured out, having Jesus in their midst demanded a celebration!

It all came to a grand, whirling, delirious climax that day known as Palm Sunday. In the weeks just preceding the great Passover Feast, Jesus had performed many spectacular miracles, climaxing with the raising of Lazarus from the dead. As crowds of pilgrims gathered in Jerusalem for the great feast, the story of that great miracle spread through the crowd like wildfire. Everywhere there was great anticipation as the people hoped that Jesus would come to Jerusalem for the festival and they would get an opportunity to see this miracle-worker up close.

Meanwhile, Jesus had been relaxing at the home of Mary and Martha and Lazarus in Bethany, a couple of miles outside the city walls. Many pilgrims found their way out to that village, hoping for a glimpse of Jesus or even of Lazarus himself. So great was the enthusiasm for Jesus that his enemies among the Pharisees and the Sanhedrin had become especially nervous and antagonistic.

Finally, on Sunday of Passover week, the news that Jesus and His disciples had set out from Bethany toward the city passed through the crowded streets like shock waves. An excited throng of pilgrims spilled out through the gates and flowed along the roadway toward Bethany in a spirit of anticipation and excitement. Somewhere along the way the two crowds met—the one crowd accompanying Jesus and His disciples from Bethany toward the city, and the other coming out from the celebration in the city to meet them. Immediately, the whole thing erupted into a grand paean of praise and celebration!

In conscious fulfillment of the prophecy of Zechariah, Jesus rode into the city on a young donkey, surrounded by His disciples and various other admirers. Perhaps at some point along the way the little donkey stumbled slightly on the loose rock which littered the winding mountain track. Someone threw down his cloak like a royal carpet to pave the way, and the gesture captured the spirit of the occasion. Yes! This was royalty! The King entering the great city of Zion to claim His throne! Running ahead, person after person threw down his cloak as well, and a spirit of excitement and celebration swept the crowd.

As the road curved over the ridge of the Mount of Olives, the people caught their first view of the ancient city. From here they could see only the southeastern corner of Jerusalem, rising terrace upon terrace from the Palace of the Maccabees and the high priest, to the great towers and magnificent gardens of Herod's palace occupying the spot on the summit believed to be the site of the original palace of King David. With them was the Son of David, this great prophet whose words of authority and acts of awesome power seemed to identify Him with the promised Messiah whom their prophets had spoken about for generations. They knew that He would be the source of their salvation.

Someone shouted, "Hosanna!"—God Saves!—and began to quote from the great 118th psalm, "Blessed is he who comes in the name of the Lord!" The crowd shouted back in the traditional antiphonal style, "Blessed is the King of Israel!" The chanting continued, "The Lord is God, and he has given us light." And the response, "Bind the festal procession with branches, up to the horns of the altar!" Branches! There were branches all around them. Someone quickly cut a palm frond from the side of the road and began to wave it as they sang. Others picked up the spirit and soon the crowd was lost in celebration, running and cheering and shouting and waving palm branches as they accompanied this remarkable man, riding quietly toward the city on His little donkey.

Apparently Jesus had had little to say until the gray-breathed Pharisees challenged this spontaneous celebration. "Teacher, rebuke your disciples!" they demanded scornfully. Jesus, I imagine, looked at them for several moments as the donkey continued to jog along the track in the midst of the crowd. Then He said reproachfully, "I tell you, if they keep quiet, the very stones will cry out." It was true, of course. Isaiah had predicted,

> For you shall go out in joy, and be led forth in peace; the mountains and the hills before you shall break forth into singing [the singing was breaking forth on those hills surrounding Jerusalem that day], and all the trees of the field shall clap their hands (Isaiah 55:12).

As the palm branches waved, it was as if the trees were indeed clapping their hands in celebration of the One who had made them and who had now come among them. There was no way for anyone who recognized Jesus to refrain from celebration!

No, the world had not grown gray from Jesus' breath. If it had grown gray at all, it was from the breath of self-appointed "holy ones" who never really understood what Jesus is all about!

Perhaps we who stand on our dignity should pause to remember who it was that protested the celebration on that first Palm Sunday. It was not those who knew the heart of God who objected, but those whose hearts had grown cold with ambition or self-importance.

Our God calls us to celebrate. As He organized His people in the wilderness before they entered into the Promised Land, God gave thorough instructions on a whole series of feasts, special celebration days designed to celebrate the goodness of the Lord. Those people knew how to celebrate! When they became established in the land and their first harvest came, God told them they were to come to Jerusalem with a special offering. Listen to what God said to them from Deuteronomy 14:26. We think of this as a book of law, a heavy burden of myriad rules and regulations, but this is what it says:

> Spend the money for whatever you desire, oxen, or sheep, or wine or strong drink, whatever your appetite craves; and you shall eat there before the LORD your God and rejoice, you and your household.

Celebrate however your heart desires, God says; just come and do it. We see a similar call to celebration in the book of Ecclesiastes, repeated several times. In chapter 5:18-20 (NIV), after looking at life, the writer says,

> Then I realized that it is good and proper for a man to eat and drink, and to find satisfaction in his toilsome labor under the sun during the few days of life God has given him—for this is his lot. Moreover, when God gives any man wealth and possessions, and enables him to enjoy them, to accept his lot and be happy in his work—this is a gift of God. He seldom reflects on the days of his life, because God keeps him occupied with gladness of heart.

God calls us to celebrate: to celebrate life, to celebrate the good things He has given us. Certainly "there is a time to weep," but there is also "a time to laugh." Certainly there is "a time to mourn," but there is also "a time to dance." As Dallas Willard says in his book, *The Spirit of the Disciplines,* "It is the act and discipline of faith to seize the season and embrace it for what it is, including the season of enjoyment."[1] Altogether too many Christians neither mourn nor dance. As far as that is true, we deserve Swinburne's epithet. In our misguided efforts to be "spiritual" and to be "pious," we have drained the color out of both our highest and our lowest moments, leaving all of life a pale gray. We have failed to seize the season and embrace it for what it really is.

You and I must understand that in our failure to celebrate the life God has given us, we dishonor the One who is its source. Let me say as clearly and as simply as I can: GOD INTENDS FOR HIS CHILDREN TO ENJOY LIFE! He intends for you and for me to enjoy the life He has given us. Of course, not everything that happens to us as Christians will bring us pleasure. But we are responsible before the Creator to savor every experience which God brings our way. We should drink as deeply of joy in the good things He gives us as we do of sorrow in a good world distorted by sin.

In his ever-popular book, *The Screwtape Letters,* told from the perspective of a demon for whom good is bad and bad good, C. S. Lewis has the senior demon, Screwtape, chide his apprentice for having allowed his "patient" to read a book he really enjoyed and take a walk in the country which filled him with joy. "Never forget," the demon says in his inverted logic, "that when we are dealing with any pleasure in its healthy and normal and satisfying form, we are, in a sense, on the Enemy's [God's] ground. I know we have won many a soul through pleasure. All the same, it is His invention, not ours. He made the pleasures: all our research so far has not enabled us to produce one."[2]

Palm Sunday teaches us that we need to learn to enjoy the good things of life which God has given, in that spirit He asks of us—hilariously. We need to learn to laugh at ourselves and to recognize that the causes we worked so feverishly to promote were perhaps not so monumental as we believed or wanted others to believe. And in that open, free celebration, perhaps we will begin to see that we do not have to subject every person to our judgments. I cannot imagine that on the day we stand before the Lord He will ask us whether we completed our job of condemning every error or failure we stumbled across. God may very well ask us whether we celebrated His gift of life and His gift of grace.

When God's people were returning to Jerusalem after the Babylonian Captivity, they were deeply grieved by their sin and the destruction it had caused. And rightly so, for they had disobeyed; they turned away from God, and the result had been disastrous. But Ezra the priest, a very legalistic man, and Nehemiah the governor, challenged them to celebrate God's grace, "for," they said, "the joy of the LORD is your strength." Certainly they wanted God's people to obey; but they recognized that it was not in that grieving that they would find their strength, but in celebration. "The joy of the LORD is your strength." It is a fact that what will sustain us and give us the motivation and the energy to continue to do the will of God is the joy we experience when we celebrate His goodness to us and His plan for us. It is indispensable for us as Christians, if we are to survive.

So I urge you to celebrate—to celebrate in worship, to celebrate when you witness to your faith, to celebrate when you pray and when you read God's Word—to recognize that the living God, the source of life, has come among us. I challenge you to celebrate with your families, to find ways at Christmas and Easter to celebrate appropriately and to say "thank you" to God for what He has done; to celebrate on Thanksgiving Day and Independence Day the gifts of the Lord; to find ways throughout the year to celebrate with your family, friends and loved ones who enjoy life with you.

I am not so sure we will win the world to Jesus Christ through condemnation. We may win them through celebration. They may be won over when they hear the mountains breaking forth with singing, the trees clapping their hands, and the joyous celebration of God's people resounding in this world. May we share that spirit of celebration as we reflect upon the triumphal entry of Jesus Christ—not only into Jerusalem, but, more broadly, into our world and, especially, into our lives.

Notes

1. Dallas Willard, *The Spirit of the Disciplines: Understanding How God Changes Lives* (San Francisco: Harper & Row, 1988), 180.

2. C. S. Lewis, *The Screwtape Letters and Screwtape Proposes a Toast* (New York: Macmillan, 1959), 41.

Good Intentions

(Mark 14)

John Mark sat bolt upright on his mattress, his heart pounding furiously. Someone was beating on the door of the gateway leading into the courtyard of his family's home, and he could hear angry voices demanding to be let in. It was after midnight, and he was fighting desperately to rouse his senses from that deep sleep into which one falls during the first few hours of the night. Downstairs, he could hear the frightened voice of the maid, Rhoda, telling his mother about the crowd of angry men carrying swords and clubs that had surrounded the house.

Young Mark quickly pulled a linen robe around his body and scrambled down the stone steps toward the entryway. Since his father's death, the young teenager had felt responsible to be the man of the family. He had no idea how he might respond to this frightening intrusion, but felt he must be at his mother's side. Mary, however, was already at the gate when he arrived, speaking coolly to the scowling sea of torch-lit faces surging about the entry.

"Yes, they were here earlier this evening," he heard her say. "We hosted them for the Paschal Supper; but they've gone. You're welcome to come in and check if you'd like, but you won't find them here. I can't tell you where they've gone." Mark recognized Judas' face, cool and impassive, at the front of the crowd. For a moment he wondered why he was not with the other disciples, but then he remembered seeing him slip out of the upper room earlier in the evening and disappear into the night. Mark had never quite trusted Judas, but he really didn't know why. Perhaps it was the way Judas ignored him and his family, always acting as if they didn't exist. By contrast, Peter always seemed glad to see him, and always asked how he was doing. In fact, since his father died, Peter had begun to take extra time to ask about his education and plans for the future, and had promised to take him fishing sometime on the Sea of Galilee.

Judas smiled blandly at Mary and said, "Thank you very much. It won't be necessary to unlock the gate. We're sorry to have disturbed you." He herded the crowd, which Mark could see included a number of temple officials, back from the gate and stood talking quietly with them for a few minutes. Then, glancing back over his shoulder at John Mark and his mother peering at them from the gate, Judas pushed his way through the throng of torches and men and led them off down the street in the opposite direction.

What was it all about? "Are they in danger, Mother?" he asked. "Why was Judas with them?" "I don't know, Mark," his mother replied. "I'm afraid they may be in danger. But I'm sure Jesus can handle it. You need to go back to bed."

But Mark was wracking his brain to try to make some sense out of this startling turn of events. Living in Jerusalem, he was aware that Jesus was not nearly so popular here as he was in the rural province of Galilee. By opening their home to him and his disciples when they were in Jerusalem, Mark's family had alienated some of the religious leaders and officials of their community. That was to be expected, his cousin Barnabas had reassured them, but Jesus was a good man and they would do well to support him.

Mark had been excited when the arrangements were made for Jesus and his disciples to meet in their home to celebrate the Passover. Their home was large, and it was not unusual for them to host guests for the great feast days; but Mark felt that never before had their roof protected so distinguished a company. They would not eat together, of course. Mark's family and a smaller group of guests would be celebrating in a different room, but they would be going through the same ritual and he could imagine each step of the familiar Passover meal. As head of the company, Jesus would begin the celebration by taking the first cup of wine and speaking the familiar benediction over it before they all partook. They would reflect on God's spectacular deliverance of their ancestors from Egypt and on his subsequent bountiful provision for them. A little later, the Head of the group would rise to begin the ritual hand washing. Later still, they would share the bitter herbs and Jesus would take one of the cakes of unleavened bread and break it, reminding them of the bread of misery they ate in Egypt and of the bread God would provide for them as free men and women.

It was not until much later that Peter told him how Jesus had unexpectedly changed the ritual that night to explain his own identity and purpose, speaking of his own death and resurrection. And He had shocked them all by washing their feet that night. Mark knew only that they had stayed late, talking. He knew because he had begged his mother to let him stay up until they left so he could see Jesus and maybe remind Peter of the promised fishing trip. When he finally heard them singing the great Hallel from the Psalms, he positioned himself to intercept them on the way out.

But when they finally emerged from the upper room, he could see that no one was in the mood for light conversation. In fact, Jesus and Peter were earnestly talking as they descended the steps, and John Mark stepped back away as the men moved toward the front entrance. "You will all fall away," Jesus was saying gravely as they passed him. "For it is written, 'I will strike the shepherd, and the sheep will be scattered.' But after I am raised up, I will go before you to Galilee."

Peter was insistent. "Even though they all fall away," he replied stubbornly, "I will not." Jesus paused at the door and turned to Peter with eyes full of compassion, yet firmness. He was silent for a moment. "Simon, Simon," he finally said with a sigh, "behold, Satan demanded to have you, that he might sift you like wheat, but I have prayed for you that your faith may not fail; and when you have turned again, strengthen your brethren."

"Lord," Peter protested, "I am ready to go with you to prison and to death."

"I tell you Peter," Jesus replied, "the cock will not crow this day, until you three times deny that you know me." But Peter was offended. Vehemently he insisted, "If I must die with you, I will not deny you." All the other disciples joined in with the same assurance. Jesus simply looked at them sadly, then turned and walked silently out into the darkness.

The disciples were firmly convinced of who Jesus was. They had seen His miracles and listened to His words and they knew He was the Christ, the Son of the Living God. Furthermore, they were absolutely committed to follow Him. They had made the decision to leave home and family and occupation to be with Him and to learn from Him. They knew they were risking unpopularity and possibly even death to be identified with Him, but they were supremely confident of their ability to withstand any temptation or threat. They would not let Him down!

If positive thinking had anything to do with their success or failure, they would surely succeed. Convinced, committed, and utterly confident, they were certain winners. But Jesus was not so sure. In fact, He knew they had drastically underestimated the deceptive power of their Enemy, as well as overestimated their own strength; and He knew that bold and confident as they were, they would surely fail. His prayer for them was that when they failed, it would not be too crushing and they would not lose their faith.

After they had gone out, John Mark continued to be greatly troubled by the conversation he had overheard. He had no idea what it all meant, of course, all this about "falling away" and "denying" Him, but clearly Jesus was anticipating some sort of trouble and did not expect the disciples to be of much help. Now, suddenly, with the latest event which had awakened him in the midnight hour, it all began to fall in place. That sinister-looking crowd of soldiers and temple police and hired thugs wielding clubs and swords were clearly after Jesus. Likely, his life was in danger! Mark realized he was the only one who knew about it. Somehow he would have to warn Jesus!

Without bothering to put on anything other than the linen robe he had pulled on when he leapt out of bed, Mark slipped out through the gate and ran down the darkened streets of the city. The arresting party already was out of sight and Mark was not sure where Jesus and His disciples had gone, but he would have to do his best. He knew they had spent several recent nights on the Mount of Olives, and though the area was large, he knew he would be most likely to find them there, outside the city walls.

Meanwhile, as he would later learn from Peter, Jesus and His disciples had gone to a small, private garden surrounded by a low stone wall on the slopes of the Mount of Olives. The disciples knew the place well. It belonged to a friend of Jesus, and they had often gone there to be away from the crowds in order to talk and pray in private. This particular night, Jesus was deeply distressed and His disciples had fallen silent as they walked with Him through the still night air. At the old stone building with the olive press which stood at the gate of the garden, Jesus asked the men to wait and pray while he took Peter and James and John with Him a little further into the garden. Peter felt his confidence begin to melt as he saw the look of anguish and distress on his Lord's face. He had never seen Him like this before.

"Please," Jesus told them, "keep alert and pray. My soul is grieved to the point of death, and I must speak with my Father about it." "Certainly! Go ahead—we'll be right here," they tried to reassure Him. The three disciples sat down and made themselves comfortable against rocks or trees, while Jesus walked a short distance away and threw Himself down on the ground in anguish. They could hear snatches of His prayer, but could not fathom what it was all about.

Anyone who has ever been very, very tired and emotionally drained can understand what happened next. Their intentions had been good; no one questioned their intentions. They absolutely meant to watch with Jesus, but the next thing they knew, He was standing over them and calling their names. Peter felt that helpless, achy feeling as if he were paralyzed and was trying to drag himself back over some great distance to consciousness. "Simon," he heard again, "are you asleep?"

"No, no! I mean, yes, I suppose I did doze off for a bit. I'm sorry! I didn't mean . . ."

"Could you not watch one hour?" Jesus replied. "Watch and pray that you may not enter into temptation; the spirit indeed is willing, but the flesh is weak."

That was certainly true, Peter had to admit. He fully intended to stay awake and be there for the Lord, but it was so hard. A few minutes later he was nodding off again.

Young John Mark, meanwhile, was picking his way through the olive groves which dotted the side of the mountain across the deep Kidron valley from the city walls. The moon was full, which was fortunate, since he had not bothered to bring a lantern. The gnarled, old olive trees cast strange, deceptive shadows across his path and he was not certain where he was. It had been foolish to think he could find a handful of men in the dark woods in the middle of the night. Besides, he was getting cold and wishing he had taken the time to put on something more substantial.

Suddenly, Mark became aware of voices not far away. Scrambling behind a tree, he listened and waited as the voices came nearer. A few moments later he could see torchlight flickering through the trees and the band of men he had last seen at his house traipsed past on the road below him. There was nothing to do now but follow them. At least they might lead him to the place where the disciples had gathered. Maybe he would be able to sprint ahead and give a warning yet.

But by the time he caught up to them, they had already surprised their prey. Some sort of scuffle had broken out and, in the ring of firelight, Mark could see Peter brandishing a sword. But Jesus stepped between him and the young man whose head was bleeding profusely, placed his hand alongside of his head and spoke quietly. As Jesus reached out toward him, several in the crowd lunged forward with weapons at the ready. Jesus turned to them with disdain.

"Have you come out as against a robber, with swords and clubs to capture me?" He asked. "Day after day I was with you in the temple teaching, and you did not seize me. But let the scriptures be fulfilled. This is your hour and the power of darkness."

Rough hands grasped at Jesus in the threatening glow of the torches as ropes were brought out to bind him. In the commotion that followed, Mark saw various disciples scrambling to get away in the darkness. Suddenly, out of nowhere, John Mark was seized from behind. In utter panic, Mark twisted and pulled to get away. The man had a tight grip on his linen robe, but Mark let it slip from his shoulders and bolted away from his would-be captor. He fled naked down the rocky pathway in terror, pursued by his own fears. At every step he was sure he heard the footfalls of his pursuers at his back. His heart pounded in his ears and his chest ached, but he didn't stop until he reached the stream at the bottom of the valley. There he finally turned to see that he was alone in the night.

Mark was ashamed of his fear. He felt he had let Jesus down. He had failed to warn Him in time and then he had run away at the first threat to his own well-being. Jesus, by contrast, had been so fearless and confident. He wished desperately that he could be more like Jesus.

A few days later he would hear the story of how Peter had failed that night. Peter had tried to reassure him that his escape was totally justifiable. Peter, on the other hand, told him how he had followed the mob to the high priest's house and then made an utter fool of himself by denying on oath that he even knew Jesus. After all his swaggering promises, Peter was crushed by his failure. He realized that he had deluded himself into believing he was stronger and more committed than any other of the disciples; the fact was that he could talk big, but when a real test came, he had neither the courage nor the strength to stand up to it.

Mark was impressed that Peter could admit this to him so frankly. It occurred to him that it took a very strong person to admit such embarrassing failures; but Peter would take no credit for any special strengths. "You want to know the only thing I have going for me, Mark?" he asked. "I'd like you to think I was a great disciple, bold and clever and strong and pious. But the only thing I have going for me is that Jesus promised to pray for me. He knows how weak I am; He knows how insensitive I am; He knows how vulnerable I am; He knows no matter how big I talk, how likely I am to fail. And He is praying for me!"

"If you don't learn anything else from this whole discouraging incident," Peter told him, "at least learn not ever to get overconfident when you are involved in spiritual warfare. Just when you think you are doing all right, you are probably more vulnerable than you can imagine. Always stay on your guard.

"That's what Jesus was trying to tell us in the garden that night," Peter concluded. "Don't ever presume you have it all together. No matter how good your intentions are, recognize that while your spirit may be willing, your flesh is weak. That's true of every one of us; our flesh is weak. We need to be alert to our weaknesses all the time. We need to submit those weaknesses to the Lord in prayer. We need to ask Him to reveal our weaknesses to us; we must depend upon Him to intercede for us and to accomplish His will—through us, if He is particularly gracious, but very likely, in spite of us. God doesn't need any more self-deluded, overconfident followers. He needs a few truly humble servants who know their limitations, and who simply place their trust in him."

Excruciating Love

(John 18:28-19:37)

Let me tell you a love story. Oh, I know what you think when someone mentions a love story. It will need to be tender and compassionate, an emotional tale of passion and tears, a romantic saga of star-crossed lovers drawn together by forces so irresistible that no cruel adversary can intervene or keep them apart. And in a way, I suppose, this is that sort of love story—although it will not seem so on the surface. For it is a harsh story, a story of undeserved and excruciating love.

As His best friend stated it, "Having loved his own who were in the world, he now showed them the full extent of his love." Jesus was abandoned into the hands of His enemies. His disciples, who loved Him and nurtured the best of intentions to stand by Him, were unprepared for the torrent of hostility which swept Him away from them. They could only stand by helplessly at a distance calculated to preserve their own lives, and watch as the raging stream of self-interest and religious pride buffeted Him about and carried Him remorselessly toward the crushing turbulence of the cross.

After their own midnight charade, in which the religious leaders found Him guilty of blasphemy for stating His true identity, the perpetrators of the arrest hustled their prisoner at daybreak on April 7, 30 A.D., to the palace of the Roman governor. They intended to eliminate this man who had challenged the foundations upon which they built their power and influence. But as subjects of a Roman colony, they had no legal authority to execute anyone. They would have to convince the governor of a capital offense against the state.

Arriving at the paved courtyard outside the Fortress of Antonia, which overlooked the temple grounds, Pilate, the Roman governor, came out to hear their charges against this accused rabble-rouser. "What charges are you bringing against this man?" Pilate asked gruffly. "If he were not a criminal," they replied, "we would not have handed him over to you." They countered his sarcasm with their own. There followed a string of spurious charges of political subversion which Pilate decided he would have to investigate for himself.

Taking Jesus inside where they would not be disturbed by the crowd, he questioned Him personally about His political agenda. It quickly became evident that Jesus' spiritual concerns, if they were a threat to the religious community, posed no apparent threat to the Roman government. So Pilate returned to the noisy crowd gathered outside to announce his verdict: "I find no basis for a charge against him."

There was an angry stir from the religious leaders responsible for the crowd. Sensing that they might not be speaking for the people, Pilate attempted to subvert their little plot. "But . . . !" he continued, holding up his hand to quiet them, "it is your custom for me to release to you one prisoner at the time of the Passover. Do you want me to release 'the king of the Jews'?"

For a number of years, the Romans had granted this concession to the cantankerous Jewish community, a token compensation for their loss of jurisdiction over capital crimes. He was giving the people the opportunity to contradict their manipulative leaders, for whom Pilate had no love. But the members of the Sanhedrin were too quick. "No, not him!" they shouted back, urging the crowd to join them, "Give us Barabbas!" (another political prisoner who had committed murder in an earlier insurrection). "Yes," the crowd shouted, "give us Barabbas!"

Pilate was unsure how to respond. The crowd had grown unruly and a riot was always a possibility with these contentious people. He really hated being manipulated by them, and he genuinely believed Jesus was innocent. Maybe he could win the sympathy of the common folks by having Jesus scourged. This punishment, which stopped just short of death, might satisfy their lust for blood and allow him to release the man without actually taking His life.

Scourging or flogging was an incredibly cruel and barbaric form of punishment. The man was stripped of his clothing and his hands were tied to an upright post. Then two soldiers approached and stood on either side with a short whip of braided leather attached to a wooden handle. Braided into the scourge were small metal balls and sharp fragments of bone. Alternately, the two soldiers would lash the back, buttocks, and legs of the victim with full force. The metal balls, sometimes curling around the chest or thighs, would cause deep bruises or contusions, while the bone fragments tore strips of flesh from the back and legs. The bones close to the surface, like those of the spine and the ribs, could be severely damaged. As the flogging continued, the thongs and bone would tear more deeply into the muscle tissue, peeling back quivering ribbons of bleeding flesh. The strength or bravery of the victim could not forestall the circulatory shock from pain and blood loss, and the flogging was calculated to bring him near death without actually killing him.[1]

It is a measure of Jesus' incredible strength and will that He was able to stand and walk about shortly after this savage beating. While they waited for the governor's next instructions, the soldiers amused themselves by putting a crown of thorns on Jesus' head and mocking Him and striking Him on the face. Eventually, Pilate led Him out to the people again, but if his sentence had been calculated to win Jesus sympathy, it had failed. As soon as the chief priests and their officials saw Him, they began to shout once more, "Crucify! Crucify!"

Pilate continued to debate with the Jewish leaders for a time until Caiaphas, the politically powerful chief priest, threatened to officially challenge his status as amicus Caesaris, or "Friend of Caesar," a standing which could either make his career or break him. Pilate finally succumbed, turning Jesus over to them to be crucified.

Sometime before noon he sent an execution squad in the charge of a centurion to the small hill of Golgotha just outside the northwest wall of the city. The upright posts (or "stipes") for the crosses already stood on the execution ground, left there from previous crucifixions. The heavy crossbeams, weighing perhaps a hundred pounds or more, normally were tied across the shoulders, the nape of the neck, and the outstretched arms of the condemned criminals, to be carried to the site of their execution. This happened that day as well, although Jesus, having been so severely beaten and being in the early stages of hypovolemic shock, struggled under the weight until a passerby was drafted to carry it for Him.

As He stood at the crucifixion site, dazed and distracted by pain, the soldiers shoved a mild drug consisting of wine and myrrh into His face. But when Jesus tasted it, He refused to drink it. He wanted to be in full possession of His senses as He experienced what was about to come. Subsequently, He was thrown to the ground and His arms were stretched out along the crossbar. Kneeling on His arm, one of the soldiers placed a seven-inch iron spike against His wrist and with several powerful blows from a large mallet, drove it between the radius and the carpals, through the various ligaments which join the wrist bones together. The spike forced the carpal bones apart, but crushed the large median nerve, sending excruciating bolts of fiery pain the length of His arm.

When he had done the same to the other arm, the soldier signaled to his comrades, and four of them, two on either end of the crossbar, dragged Jesus' body to the vertical stipes and hoisted the beam into place while Jesus bit His lip in pain. Shoving his shoulder beneath Jesus' knees, one burly soldier held his feet, one atop the other, against the upright beam while another soldier drove a third spike through the instep between the second and third metatarsals, pinning His feet to the cross. Once again the pain was excruciating as the nail smashed through the deep peroneal nerve. The location of each of the spikes driven through His body was calculated to avoid major damage to arteries, thus limiting blood loss and prolonging the torturous procedure.

Their work complete, the soldiers nailed the charges Pilate had printed on a small sign to the top of the cross and sat down to wait for Jesus' death, along with that of the two criminals crucified on either side of Him. A number of the religious leaders began to mock Him, while Caiaphas stood by to hear His confession and offer Him absolution. But Jesus was the only high priest God would hear that day, and He prayed for them, saying between tortured breaths, "Father, forgive them, for they know not what they do."

Breathing was indeed a major effort on the cross. Hanging by the arms in that contorted position, one could not get enough oxygen and would periodically have to push up on the feet. This, of course, would place the entire weight of the body on the damaged tarsals and produce searing pain in the feet and legs. It would also force the wrists to rotate on the squared spikes, sending fiery pain along the injured median nerves; and it would rub the shredded back along the rough, slivered upright beam of the cross. Muscle cramps would increasingly wrench the body, and every effort at breathing would become agonizing.

Even in the midst of this agony, Jesus was aware of what was going on around Him. Spotting His mother close by, He realized that she would have cut herself off from His skeptical brothers by this act, and possibly from any material support as a widow. His faithful disciple, John, also stood by, and Jesus called out to them from the cross, commending each to the other's care. Whether any of the other disciples had the courage to be identified with Jesus at this critical moment is doubtful, but a number of the women who had accompanied Him on some of His ministry through Galilee and Judea were there, and Jesus appreciated their unsung courage.

For all His physical torment, however, you and I cannot come close to perceiving the level of His spiritual torment. Jesus' greatest agony came from His sense of abandonment by God. Having lived His entire life surrounded by the reassuring love and power of His heavenly Father, Jesus was now left to stare into that black hole left by the departure of everything good He had ever known. He was now experiencing the absolute despair of abandonment by God, the payment of all sinners left to face the wrath of God on their own.

"My God, my God, why hast thou forsaken me," He cried out with deep, wrenching spasms of unimaginable pain. "Why art thou so far from helping me, from the words of my groaning?" He continued quoting from Psalm 22. Those who were watching gathered around to hear His words. Spoken in Aramaic, "Eloi, Eloi, lamasabach-thani," they thought He was calling out to Elijah. "He's calling for Elijah to come and help him. Let's see if Elijah comes to take him down." There was a round of crude laughter. "All who see me mock at me," Jesus continued to recite the astonishingly prophetic psalm. "I am poured out like water, and all my bones are out of joint . . . my strength is dried up like a potsherd, and my tongue cleaves to my jaws."

"He's thirsty. Bring the sop with the vinegar," someone shouted. Jesus struggled for another breath. The pain racked His body. Somehow the words of that remarkable psalm, one He had learned at His mother's knee, brought Him a measure of solace in the midst of His pain: "They have pierced my hands and feet—I can count all my bones—they stare and gloat over me; they divide my garments among them, and for my raiment they cast lots."

He would cling to the implicit promise of this psalm, even in the midst of His devastating pain. "But thou, O Lord, be not far off! O thou my help, hasten to my aid!" There was a deep, unspeakable comfort in the words of Scripture which He had learned so long ago.

As the afternoon wore on, many of the spectators had tired and gone home. The high priests, too, had gone. They had had to return to the temple to help with preparations for this special Sabbath passover. For several hours they would be slaughtering lambs brought by individual families for their Paschal sacrifice. How little did they know that the real sacrifice toward which each of those petty sacrifices pointed was even at that very moment hanging on the cross—God's own sacrifice for even their sins! Jesus was on the cross at the very hour the Paschal lambs were being sacrificed in the temple.

Jesus was intimately familiar with the scene which would be reenacted in countless Jewish homes that evening, even as His life slipped away. As families gathered around their tables on this Sabbath eve, the fathers would begin the celebration with the Sabbath blessing which renewed the memory of the Seventh Day of Creation. Jesus remembered the words of that blessing, and His parched lips moved almost silently to repeat them:

> Thus the heaven and the earth were finished and all the host of them. And on the seventh day God finished his work which he had done, and he rested on the seventh day from all his work . . . [which he had created through (His Word) his logos] (Genesis 2:1-2).

God finished the work which He had begun . . . the excruciating work of redemption, for which Jesus had been laboring now for some six hours on the cross. In a moment of incredible relief, Jesus knew His work was complete. "It is finished," He said softly.

Even as He spoke, the clear sound of the trumpets from the temple rang out across the hillside, calling the people to evening prayers. With His final, agonizing breaths, Jesus also repeated the prayer all Israel was praying in ignorance at that hour: "In thy hand are the souls of the living and the dead. . . . Into thy hands I commend my spirit, thou hast redeemed me, O Lord, thou God of truth." But in His agony on the cross, Jesus prayed it as He had learned it in childhood, "Abba, into thy hands I commit my spirit." His mother, who had long before taught Him this very prayer, was standing at a distance and listened. "And having said this, he breathed his last."

As Mary wept in Jesus' arms, the Jewish leaders came to the soldiers with a request. They wanted the bodies down before the Sabbath began. Would they kindly break the legs of these criminals and end the ordeal? Breaking the legs, of course, would make it impossible for the criminals to push up and breathe, thus leading to their asphyxiation. The soldiers complied, breaking the legs of the two thieves with a swift blow of the mallet; but when they came to Jesus, they saw He was already dead. Just to make sure, one of them thrust his spear into the chest cavity in a precise maneuver familiar to soldiers. The sharp point of the spear found its mark, for there was a sudden gush of blood and water, indicating that the pericardium surrounding the heart had been punctured, releasing a clear, watery fluid, followed by a rush of blood released when the distended wall of the heart was perforated. There could be no doubting the ordeal was over.

John, for one, would never be the same. Here was the man they had called one of the "sons of thunder" for his volatile temperament—the man who had offered to call down fire from heaven on Jesus' enemies. Here was the man who had contended with the other disciples for the place of honor at Jesus' right hand. But what he had seen this day would humble him and change him utterly and forever. He had seen an astonishing display of love, a willingness to suffer unbelievable anguish on behalf of those He loved. John knew Jesus might have avoided this suffering at any time. But He had not avoided it. Indeed, He had invited it.

John was only beginning to see how this was fitting in with a much larger and more comprehensive plan of God to offer a disintegrating world a chance for wholeness. He was only beginning to see how Jesus' act of unparalleled love was the fulfillment of Isaiah's prophecy about the suffering servant:

Surely he has borne our griefs and carried our sorrows; yet we esteemed him stricken, smitten by God, and afflicted. But he was wounded for our transgressions, he was bruised for our iniquities; upon him was the chastisement that made us whole, and with his stripes we are healed (Isaiah 53:4-5).

The bruises and stripes were clearly those Jesus had received from the lash of his tormentors, and in some mysterious way, He had suffered the penalty for our sins in His anguish on the cross.

But what John remembered more than anything else were the words Jesus had spoken just before this horrible ordeal. He had told His followers: "My command is this: Love each other as I have loved you. Greater love has no one than this, that one lay down his life for his friends."

It was no soft love story. It was a terribly hard, terribly costly, but terribly substantial love which Jesus had demonstrated. It was a love which challenged John to put away his rigid, judgmental spirit and love even those who disagreed with him—even those who contended with him, even those who persecuted him. It was a love which challenged John to put away his religious pride and his dreams of authority and prestige and honor to become a servant to every person the Lord set in his pathway.

It was an awesome love, an excruciating love—literally, from the Latin excruciatus, or "out of the cross." I wonder—is there any place in the church today where a lost world can see such love?

Note

1. This and subsequent references to the crucifixion are primarily drawn from William D. Edwards, Wesley J. Gabel, Floyd E. Hosmer, "On the Physical Death of Jesus Christ," *Journal of the American Medical Association,* vol. 255, no. 11 (March 21, 1986): 455-1463.

Coming to Believe

(John 19:38-20:31)

The disciples were stunned. How could it have happened? Oh, they knew following Jesus was a risk. They knew the religious establishment was antagonistic toward Jesus' unorthodox approach. They even knew political uprisings were often brutally put down. But here was the man who had walked on water—they were witnesses—the man who had healed the sick and raised the dead. And He had such a following! The city had been all agog a week earlier, celebrating Jesus' entry into Jerusalem as if He were a king.

And now His body hung on that awful cross, His back shredded from the flogging, the nerves and ligaments in His wrists and feet torn by rough iron spikes. If they had held out any hope that He would miraculously step down from the cross after suffering this horrible humiliation, it had ended when the soldier ruptured His heart with a spear point.

John, standing by with Jesus' mother, was sick. There seemed to be nothing he could do but watch this wretched drama play out to its bitter end. At least he could clap his hands and frighten away the huge carrion birds which periodically settled toward the cross. He didn't know what they were going to do next. He didn't know if they would throw Jesus' body into a pauper's grave or what, but he wanted to stay until he found out. Finally, after the three bodies had hung motionless on the crosses for quite some time with no attempt to breathe, the soldiers, knowing it was finished, began their cleanup. John recognized two men approaching Jesus' cross along with their servants. They were members of the

Jewish ruling council whom John knew to be sympathetic with Jesus' cause. They spoke for a few moments with the centurion, showing him some official-looking papers (which John later learned they had obtained from Pilate), giving them permission to take Jesus' body.

The soldiers worked alternately, using huge iron pincers and bracing themselves against the base of the cross, to remove the long iron spike from Jesus' feet. Then they helped to lower the crossbar to the ground with Jesus' slowly stiffening body still attached. It was gruesome work, prying the other two spikes out of the crossbar and finally extracting them from Jesus' wrists, but eventually it was done. Now the two men and their servants quickly wrapped Jesus' body in a clean linen cloth and carried it away. John probably took Mary back with him to the home of John Mark, but the other women followed and watched as Joseph of Arimathea had Jesus' body brought to his own tomb, hewn out of a rocky hillside in a garden plot he owned nearby.

From a distance, Mary Magdalene and another Mary, the mother of Joses, watched as the men hurried in and out of the tomb, tearing long strips of cloth in which to wrap the body for burial in the traditional custom. They could not see all that was happening, and knew that the rush was to complete the burial before sundown and the beginning of the Sabbath. Unsure whether the men had time to prepare the body properly, they agreed to come with additional spices when the Sabbath was over, to complete the work in case it had been done hastily.

But in fact, Joseph and his helpers had wrapped Jesus' body carefully in many layers of linen cloth, distributing some seventy-five pounds of spices—mainly myrrh and aloes—between the folds of cloth. They had also wrapped His head in the customary Oriental fashion, with a series of spirals, leaving the face and neck uncovered. Now the body lay, mummy-like, on a stone shelf along the wall. With no time to linger, the men pushed and levered the great stone into place over the mouth of the tomb and headed back into the city, followed by the women.

Since nearly all the men and women who traveled with Jesus were from Galilee, they would have spent this special Passover Sabbath with friends or family living in Jerusalem. But none were in the mood for celebrating. They were in shock, trying to grasp the dimensions of the tragedy which had befallen them. And might their own lives be in jeopardy? None of them joined in the services at the synagogue that Sabbath. Each withdrew into himself, gripped by a deep, personal sense of despair. They had no idea where to go from here. They had simply been following Jesus. They had committed their lives to Him, and now suddenly He was gone. He had left them virtually no instructions and in any case, He personally had been the focus of their mission. Without Him, there was nothing left.

Meanwhile, some of the chief priests and Pharisees, anxious that their plan to stifle this miracle worker might still somehow come unraveled, remembered that Jesus had spoken obscurely of rising from the dead; so they decided the possibility of fraud was great enough that they would have to break the Sabbath to place a guard at the tomb, so the disciples couldn't steal the body and try to convince people that Jesus was still alive. Impatient for the whole unpleasant episode to end, Pilate granted a contingent of Roman soldiers, who went with a group of the religious leaders to the tomb, undoubtedly checking to make sure the body was where they had been told it would be. They then sealed the tomb and posted a guard.

The Sabbath passed without incident. Just before sunrise on the first day of the week, the women gathered up their spices and slipped out of the house where they had been staying. The city gates would open at dawn, and they hoped they could get to the tomb, add their spices, and be away before anyone came asking questions. Jesus' mother, physically and emotionally exhausted by the devastating events of the previous days, finally slept. John watched the women disappear up the street, reflecting for a moment on the therapeutic value of having something to do when you are overwhelmed by grief. He was glad Jesus had asked him to care for His mother. When Peter knocked apologetically at the gate a little later, John was glad to have a companion, someone to talk with or just sit with and share his sorrow.

As the women neared the garden, the reality of the tragedy they had witnessed seemed to weigh upon them more heavily with each step—the images of Jesus on that cross, suffering an agonizing death. They were not even sure if they really wanted to see His face, distorted now by suffering. As those who had watched the entombment described what they had seen, they realized they would not be able to move the stone without help, and wondered if the gardener or anyone else would be stirring that early.

But as they approached the little garden outside the wall of Jerusalem, to their great surprise and dismay, they saw that the tomb stood open. A quick look inside revealed it to be empty. While the other women waited at the tomb, Mary Magdalene ran back along the way they had come to tell the others. Arriving back at the home of John Mark, breathless and excited, she found John and Peter talking and rushed up to them exclaiming, "They have taken the Lord out of the tomb, and we don't know where they have laid him!" As Peter and John tried to get the story straight, several more of the women rushed in, their eyes wide with excitement. They interrupted each other with descriptions of angels and earthquakes and guards and graveclothes, but none of it made any sense to the bewildered apostles. Trying to calm their informers, John assured them that he and Peter would check it out, and the two men eased themselves through the excited group of women, turning and running the moment they were outside the gate.

When they reached the tomb, they found it open as the women had described, though they saw no angels or distracted guards. In the stillness, they stepped inside. There, on the shelf carved out of the wall of the tomb, Peter and John saw the evidence that first opened their eyes to something they could not previously conceive. The graveclothes which had tightly bound Jesus' body lay there on the stone ledge—but there was no one inside! Under the weight of seventy-five pounds of spices, the mummy shape had simply collapsed! No one had unwound it. In fact, the headpiece lay still intertwined (the Greek word says), a short gap separating it from the strips which had shaped themselves around the body.

It was incontrovertible evidence. There was no other explanation. No one could have removed the body without disturbing the graveclothes. As they stood there in wonder, they realized that when Jesus had spoken of resurrection, He was not speaking merely about some spiritual regeneration in the future; He had been speaking about His body actually materializing in a new and living form. It wasn't even that His old body had revived and started breathing again, like that of Lazarus (who had to be helped in removing the graveclothes). No, Jesus' body had passed through the graveclothes as if nothing in the physical world presented any barrier. He had simply risen and gone away!

Still bewildered, but greatly encouraged, Peter and John left the tomb to find the other disciples. A short while after they left,

Mary Magdalene returned by herself, weeping in confusion and grief. She had missed the earlier appearance of the angels and could make no sense out of the missing body. It seemed to her a cruel hoax. But she would be the first to receive the ultimate confirmation of Jesus' resurrection, for while she stumbled about in her tears, Jesus appeared. Quite unlike the distorted body which she had seen removed from the cross a few days before, and which she expected to see in the tomb, Jesus looked virile, strong and healthy. For a moment she mistook Him for the gardener they had earlier hoped to find. But then He spoke her name and she dissolved in tears of joy and amazement.

By evening, most of the disciples had gathered at John Mark's house. They were still frightened of the authorities and had gathered secretly, making sure all the doors and gates were locked and barred. Again and again they reviewed the events of the day in wonder and disbelief. What did it all mean? Had Jesus disappeared and returned to heaven? Several more of the women had claimed to see Jesus before the day was over, but the men were skeptical. They were not sure the women weren't having some sort of hysterical visions. Then around dinnertime, two other followers of Jesus (Cleopas and quite possibly Luke) rushed in independently with their own story. They had been walking along the road to Emmaus when Jesus appeared to them. Each witness was credible—but how could it all be true?

As they talked, suddenly a familiar voice sounded through the room. "Shalom!" (Peace be with you). The voices died away and in stunned amazement they turned to the speaker. The doors had been shut and locked, but here He was, standing in their midst! They were terrified. If He were a vision, He certainly seemed a substantial one. "Why are you troubled, and why do doubts rise in your minds?" Jesus asked them. "Look at my hands and my feet. It is I myself!"

Yes, they saw Him, or at least something that looked like Him. But no one moved. Jesus continued, "Touch me and see; a ghost does not have flesh and bones, as you see I have." When He had said this, He showed them His hands and feet. And while they still did not believe because of joy and amazement, He asked them, "Do you have anything here to eat?" In response they gave Him a piece of broiled fish (I can picture one of the disciples edging over to Him with this fish by the tail) and He took it and ate it in their presence.

Everything here was calculated to provide for the disciples the tangible evidence they would need in order to embrace the truth of the resurrection. Jesus wanted them to know for certain that He had risen from the dead. He wanted them to know for certain that they were not having some sort of hysterical vision. They could touch Him; they could put their fingers in the hole in His wrist, or their hands in His side; they could watch that fish disappear as He ate it. Jesus knew how difficult it would be for them to grasp this truth. He hadn't even tried to explain it to them in advance, for He knew they could never grasp the concept of a resurrection. They would have to see it firsthand if they were going to believe it.

When Thomas, who was not there that first evening, asked for equally tangible proof, the Lord gave it to him. He even used Thomas's own words to give him a little additional proof. He said, "Put your finger here. You asked about it last week, remember? So put your finger here; put your hand in my side. And stop doubting and believe." There was no reproof in Jesus' remarks. Thomas, after all, was not the only one who found it difficult to believe. They all doubted. Jesus was intent upon convincing them all, for He had just introduced something totally new into His creation. These eyewitnesses would be the ones commissioned with the task of convincing others who would not be there to see it firsthand. "Because you have seen me, you have believed," Jesus told them. "Blessed are those who have not seen and yet have believed." He was thinking about *you.*

For the men and women who witnessed the resurrection, convincing others became the compelling motivation for their lives. Two thousand years later, the story is still being told. John tells us his goal was to convince everyone who would hear his words or read his account that the Author of Life itself had visited this planet and was offering eternal life and victory over death to all who would believe and place their trust in Him. God had not required him, nor does He require us, to take a blind leap of faith to believe something that seems utterly unbelievable. He had been willing to provide tangible evidence to prove that the entire episode of Jesus' life was in fact the personal interaction of God with His creation. He wanted not only those first disciples to know that; He also wanted you and me to know that. He wanted us to hear the testimony of those who were there, who placed their hands in Jesus' side and came to believe.

Everything else would flow from this fundamental truth concerning the identity of Jesus Christ. The apostle Paul would later introduce his great theological treatise to the Romans with the observation that Jesus was proved to be the literal Son of God by the power exhibited in His resurrection from the dead. Everything else about salvation that Paul tells us comes from this fact, fundamentally established by the resurrection of Jesus. The validity of all Jesus' teaching would be established by the reality of His indestructible life.

What John probably could not see (he was too close to it) was that the most compelling evidence of the resurrection is the way in which the disciples' utter conviction of its truth so dramatically changed their own lives. These men who had followed Jesus so loyally, but who had no idea which way to turn when He was gone; these men who had such good intentions, but who had run away the moment they were challenged; these men who had hidden in an upper room, fearing to believe what seemed to them the wild tales of hysterical women; in the end they were so utterly convinced of Jesus' resurrection from the dead that it became the sole content of their preaching. Everywhere they went they preached the resurrection of Jesus Christ from the dead. It motivated them to launch a mission that would change the world and continues to change the world to this day. And at the last, each would boldly and without regret sacrifice his own life to defend the truth of what he had seen and heard. They were utterly convinced. Jesus made certain they were utterly convinced. They had come to believe.

They offer us a compelling testimony. Our lives too can be transformed. "Blessed," Jesus says, "are those who have not seen and yet have believed." The very fact that we celebrate Sunday mornings is evidence of that belief, for it was Sunday morning after Jesus' resurrection that the disciples came together and He first met with them. It was such an astonishing fact that for two thousand years those who have come to believe in Jesus have met together on the first day of the week in commemoration of that resurrection which changed their lives and changed the world.

Has the time come for you to set aside your skepticism and embrace the truth which will give meaning and direction to your life? That is what it did for those first disciples. That is what it always does. It is the resurrection which will give your life purpose and hope. And ultimately it is the resurrection which will take you beyond the grave to experience the wonder and joy of life in His name.

But only you can make the decision to embrace the Living Christ; or, in rejecting Him, obstinately persist along the pathway which leads into the grave, but not beyond.

Feed My Sheep

(John 21:1-19)

Three days of walking from the rough, rocky limestone out-croppings which surround Jerusalem will bring one to the gentle, grass-covered hills which cradle that lovely blue gem of a lake known as the Sea of Galilee (or alternatively, Chinnereth, Gennesaret, or Tiberius). It was in this exquisite setting that a number of the disciples, including Peter, James, and John, had plied their trade of fishing in the early days prior to Jesus' call to discipleship. Indeed, it was on the shores of this very lake where Jesus had called Peter and his brother, Andrew, and James and John to be His disciples.

Thus it is not surprising that after the dramatic and confusing events of Jesus' death and resurrection, these disciples were only too glad to escape the hostile environment of the city of Jerusalem and head for this place, which held such warm and peaceful memories. Back at the lake and uncertain of what the future held for them, the seven disciples mentioned in John 21 found themselves drawn to the secure and familiar ritual of fishing. In response to Peter's suggestion, they borrowed a boat—probably from a relative still involved in the fishing trade—caught the westerly breeze which rises in the evening, and slipped out onto the lake with their nets.

All that night under the stars one could hear the homely, comfortable sounds of oars thumping on the wooden sides of the boat, the gentle lapping of the water, the low, muffled voices of the men, and the periodic splash of the net being thrown out into the water. But they caught nothing. It must have occurred to Peter during the night that there was a certain parallel between their failure this night and their failure the night before Jesus had called him to become a disciple.

In any case, as they neared the shore toward morning, with the dawn lighting the sky behind them and the cool shadows still lying on the pebbly beach a hundred yards or so ahead, they saw the figure of a man and heard His voice carry easily across the water, asking if they had caught any fish. When they told Him "No," He directed them to cast the net on the right side of the boat where He assured them they would find some. Now you and I, knowing who this stranger is, are not surprised when they find the net so full of fish they cannot pull it into the boat. We have heard this story before. But up to this point the disciples are afraid to get their hopes up too high.

Now, however, John turns to Peter and says, "It is the Lord!" Immediately, impetuous Peter leaps over the side of the boat and begins to swim to shore. It is not hard to picture him emerging from the water, his clothes dripping and his hair plastered against his head, expressions of awe and delight alternating across his astonished face as he looks into the face of Jesus. The others are right behind him, beaching the boat and clambering out onto the rocks, only to stand in silent amazement, gaping at their master and the charcoal fire over which fish and bread were heating.

Jesus finally breaks the stunned silence by inviting them to bring some of the fish they have just caught. Peter, his reverie broken, rushes back out to the boat to pull in the net which they later discover contains an awesome tally of 153 large fish. Jesus invites them to join Him for breakfast, and we can only imagine the excited conversation which must have followed as the disciples questioned Jesus about His whereabouts and experiences over the past few days and weeks.

After breakfast, as the group sat around the fire, Jesus turned very deliberately to Peter and asked, "Simon, son of John, do you love me more than these?" Without seeing His eyes or the motion of His hands, it is hard for us to know what Jesus was referring to when He said "more than these." Was He asking if Peter loved Him more than he loved the other disciples? Was He asking if Peter loved Him more than he loved the boats and nets and fish to which they seemed to be returning? But as we watch the drama play out with three opportunities for Peter to affirm his love for the Lord, we recognize that Jesus is giving Peter a chance to redeem himself for the three denials of his affiliation with Jesus at the time of His crucifixion.

And then we remember something else. We remember that on that occasion Peter had boasted that even if all the other disciples forsook Jesus and fled, he would not. He would be there. He would be with Him. He would risk anything. He would risk his very life to be with Jesus, if necessary. No matter if the others failed, Peter would not. I believe Jesus is asking Peter, "Today, this morning, are you still willing to boast that you love me more than the rest of the disciples love me? Are you willing to take a greater risk than the other disciples are willing to take? Do you love me more than these?" Even Jesus' form of address, "Simon, son of John"—He does not call him Peter or Rock here—seems to remind Peter that he, like all the others, is a natural man, a man of dust, born in the common way and subject to common failures.

Jesus is not trying to humiliate Peter. Jesus is fully aware of Peter's potentially powerful witness. But He knows that Peter will never reach his optimum potential if he does not start with a realistic self-assessment, something so difficult for all of us to do. In his response, Peter drops the earlier comparison with the other disciples and replies quite simply, "Yes, Lord; you know that I love you."

Commentators have debated this, but there may be some significance in John's choice of words here. Granting that the discussion may have taken place in Aramaic where the distinction between words is not quite as strong, John keeps contrasting two Greek words we have come to know for love, *agape* and *phileo*. He very purposefully includes one word and then the other. *Agape* is a very strong word which describes a selfless devotion at any cost, a willingness to risk anything for the object of that love. *Phileo*, on the other hand, generally describes a genuine but less noble affection and honor. What Jesus actually asks is, "Peter, do you *agape* me?" And Peter says, "Well, I can honestly say I *phileo* you." Jesus is asking about this highest form of love, the kind of love that Peter had expressed before his denial, and Peter responds with a much less overwhelming word. He replies, "Well, I do have a great and deep affection and concern for you."

Jesus is asking, "Peter, can you still say that you have a completely selfless, self-sacrificing love for me which supersedes that of all other men and which will allow you to take any risk on my behalf? Can you say that honestly to me, Peter?"And Peter replies, "In all honesty, I can only say that I have a deep and abiding affection for you. I would like it to be more, I wish it were more, but I am not certain that I have within me the resources to love you as you have loved me. I have seen agape in you. I promised to risk my life for you, but you gave up yours for me instead, and I cannot speak more highly of my qualifications to be your servant."

Jesus' reply is a compassionate affirmation of Peter's honesty and commitment. He says in effect, "That is sufficient for now. I can use you to feed my lambs." He commissions him at this point to feed His little lambs. I can imagine Peter's gaze turned down as he poked at the fire with a stick. He is overwhelmed with a sense of his own inadequacy. But Jesus' gaze is still fixed upon him; He knows what is taking place in his heart. And a second time He says, "Simon, son of John, do you truly love me?" And again He uses the word *agape.* He wants to make certain Peter grasps His point. But Peter can only reply as he did the first time, "Yes, Lord; you know that I *phileo* you." Jesus says again, "Tend my sheep."

Peter is still overwhelmed by his inadequacy. He still cannot quite look the Lord in the face, even though He has given him this significant commission. After more awkward moments pass, the other disciples waiting in sympathetic silence, Jesus says a third time, "Simon, son of John, do you love me?" And this time Jesus uses the word *phileo*, which is really a very wonderful word, expressing a deep and genuine compassion and concern for another person. Jesus asks, "Do you have that kind of love for me, Peter?"

Peter is grieved because Jesus said, "Do you *phileo* me?" He knows that Jesus knows what is going on in his heart. And he looks up at Jesus with deep sadness and remorse and says with great emotion, "Lord, you know everything; you know that I *phileo* you."

And Jesus looks deeply into his anguished eyes and says in effect, "Are you listening to me, Peter? I do know that about you, and I want you to feed my ·sheep." He is saying, "Peter, I know who you are; but because you know who you are and because you are grieved by your own failure and your own inadequacy, and because you have sincerely given your heart to me, I do know I can trust you with my sheep. Do you hear me, Peter? I am saying that I can trust you with my sheep in spite of your failures, in spite of your humanness." He goes on to suggest that Peter's commission will be a costly one, but He knows and believes that Peter is willing to pay the price. He concludes, "Follow Me"—Pattern your life after Me, Peter, and you will know something both of the cost and of the reward of service.

It is interesting at this point that Peter blurts out, "Well, what about John?" Jesus replies, "We're not talking about John, Peter. We are talking about you. You heard my call. What I say to John is not your concern. Your concern is what I say to you. I am asking you to follow Me. And whatever the cost is for you, Peter, I want you to follow Me. I don't care if anyone else understands that. I don't care if anyone else heard Me call you. You need to follow Me."

That call comes to you and me as well. It does not come because we are greatly talented, nor because we have maintained a flawless spiritual record during our lifetime, nor because we know everything there is to know about the Truth, nor because we have been blessed with a winning self-confidence. The call comes to us just as it came to Peter.

Imagine Him looking into your eyes, calling you by name, fixing you in His gaze and saying, "Do you love Me? I trust you to feed My sheep, because you know who you are. You know that despite your failures I am your only source of adequacy, and I have called you and you must be willing to follow Me."

Can you say, "Yes, Lord, you know that I love you"?

Where in the World Is Jesus?

(Acts 1:1-11)

"T minus 10 . . . 9 . . . 8 . . . 7 . . ." I remember it as if it were last week. I can still hear the voice crackling in the microphone: "6 . . . 5 . . . 4 . . ." I can feel the electricity in the air, the tension building in the pit of my stomach: "3 . . . 2 . . . 1 . . . IGNI-TION! We have ignition!"

A brilliant, white-hot flame erupted under the 363-foot high Saturn V rocket, still gripped by enormous steel clamps as 7.5 million pounds of thrust built up beneath this thirty-six-story sky-scraper. Then the restraining structure fell back and with a tremendous roar the Apollo 11 space craft lifted out of billowing clouds of smoke to hurtle three men—Neil Armstrong, "Buzz" Aldrin, and Michael Collins—toward the moon. Five days later, on July 20, 1969, they set foot where only science fiction writers had dared to dream. It was "one giant leap for mankind" to tran-scend the gravity which had bound our ancestors to this earth for thousands of years since we first burrowed into the surface of the planet. Without question, this escape from the confines of the earth is one of the most exciting and significant events of this cen-tury, and will be remembered and treated as such by generations to come, as long as the human race continues.

Thus it is both surprising and curious that an event every bit as remarkable—the ascension of Christ—generates so little atten-tion, even among those closest to it.

You may think it is rather silly to compare the ascension of Christ to a moon launch. But there are some striking similarities. Both were historic firsts; both achieved some sort of freedom from the restraints of earth. If anything, the ascension of Christ is the more remarkable, as it seems to involve none of the known laws of physics.

Yet considering how remarkable the ascension must have been, it generated very little interest—only a few Renaissance paintings of Jesus, draped in robes and sandals, floating away awkwardly into the sky. The whole image never seemed terribly credible, particularly to the skeptic who has always seen Christianity as hopelessly steeped in first-century mythology. The real focus of the first-century Christians was always on the resurrection, not on the ascension. If anything, the ascension was seen as a natural extension of the resurrection.

It was the resurrection that caught people's attention and imagination. It was at the resurrection that everything in the cosmos changed. It was here that death was defeated and the effects of death reversed. It was here that the kingdom of God was displayed in power, and it was here that Jesus received a new body unaffected by the former restrictions of earth. Therefore, the ascension was apparently not much of a surprise to anyone who understood that Jesus had a new, glorified body.

Still, the ascension is an important and significant thing. It tells us something very important, because it answers the question: Where did Jesus go? He was, after all, flesh and blood like you and me. He walked the surface of this planet as we do. Where did He go when His life here was complete? Perhaps more importantly, where in the world is Jesus today?

Both questions have an impact upon how we look at our life as well as our death. Of all the Gospel writers, Luke alone tells us about it. In fact, Luke gives us two accounts of the ascension, one to close his Gospel and one at the opening of the book of Acts. This is very intentional and gives us a huge clue to the way in which Luke understood the events he recorded in Acts. He uses the ascension as his transition from the life of Jesus in the Gospels to the life of Jesus in the early church.

"In my former book, Theophilus," he begins, referring to the Gospel of Luke which he also addressed to this unknown man, perhaps an intelligent representative of the Roman middle-class, "I wrote about all that Jesus began to do and to teach until the day He was taken up to heaven." Now, that is a rather odd sentence unless he wants to imply that Jesus continued to teach and to do things after He was "taken up to heaven." Throughout Luke's second book, we witness the acts of the Holy Spirit. Many people have suggested that the "Acts of the Apostles" should be more appropriately called "The Acts of the Holy Spirit." But at the same time, we sense Christ's abiding presence. We sense the energy of Jesus filling the book and indeed the whole succeeding story of God's people on earth. All people, all Christians throughout the ages, have had that sense of Jesus' presence. Though we cannot see Him, we have a strong sense of His presence with us.

Jesus had begun to do something tremendously significant within His creation. Clearly it would not end with His death or even His resurrection. But how would He continue what He had begun to do and to teach?

The disciples were beginning to learn that they would have a significant role in this mission, whatever it was. Jesus had commissioned them to make new disciples for Himself throughout the world. But He had also promised to accompany them in this venture—"And lo, I am with you always, to the very end of the age." But how did Jesus intend to fulfill that promise?

His first task, after His death and resurrection, was a very pragmatic one—to convince His disciples beyond a doubt that He was alive. That was as hard for them to accept as it would have been for us. So for forty days He appeared to them in various places and ways, showing them the scars on His body, talking with them about familiar things, even eating food to convince them He was not a ghost or a figment of their imagination. They needed to be convinced that He had conquered death, that He was indeed alive, before they were ready to go on. That was Jesus' first goal after His resurrection.

But if the disciples knew Jesus was alive, if they understood His message, if they accepted their responsibility to make disciples for His new kingdom, the fact remained that they had to feel totally inadequate to the task. They were, after all, a tiny minority of uneducated, inexperienced persons of no reputation or influence in a powerful pagan society. Jesus had unique powers to move the multitudes, but they did not. What would they do without Him? How could they ever accomplish this overwhelming task if Jesus were not with them? All of them hoped against hope that He would now stay with them and give direction and power to their mission. They were happy to follow Him, but without Him they knew themselves to be powerless. And there was a significant element of fear motivating the disciples in the days following the resurrection.

What Jesus had in mind they did not yet fully grasp. So on one occasion, Jesus told them, "Do not leave Jerusalem, but wait for the gift my Father promised, which you have heard me speak about. For John baptized with water, but in a few days you will be baptized with the Holy Spirit."

Jesus called upon them to testify to the things they had seen and heard concerning Him in those few years they had walked with Him, and to call others to follow Him. But He also was informing them that He intended to equip them with a special power to undertake this task: the power of the Holy Spirit.

In Acts 1:6, the disciples ask if Jesus is now going to restore the long-awaited kingdom to Israel. They were still confused about what He was trying to do. In earlier days they had been captivated by the thought that they would have positions of power and authority in a politically restored Israel—something the whole nation of Israel had dreamed of for centuries. But Jesus says, "Sorry to disappoint you. This is another matter you don't really need to know about right now." And, indeed, they do drop the subject and we do not hear them concerned about that again. They are about to be initiated into a spiritual kingdom which will completely preoccupy them for the rest of their days.

Theirs would be a far greater power, aimed at a far nobler end than any political power. When the Holy Spirit had filled them they would receive a heavenly power, one which would equip them to accomplish mighty deeds and to share a compelling message which would transform the world in spite of their own weaknesses and limitations. We see that spectacular power at work throughout the book of Acts.

This is where our consideration of the first few verses of Acts often ends. But at this moment a very peculiar thing happens. Luke tells us, "After he said this [after His final words of challenge to His disciples], he was taken up before their very eyes, and a cloud hid him from their sight." The disciples are curious, but they do not seem terribly disturbed by what they have seen. After all, they are becoming used to Jesus appearing and disappearing.

As it happens, this is the last time these disciples will see Him on earth. It is not, however, the last time He will appear. It is interesting that Stephen describes actually seeing Him "standing at the right hand of God." He does not call this a vision. The apostle Paul tells of Jesus appearing to him, and in his letter to the Corinthians he lists it right along with the resurrection appearances which happened before his ascension. Others, like Ananias, speak very naturally of conversations with Jesus long after He had left the earth. Wherever it is that Jesus has gone, He doesn't seem to be very far away.

It is a significant question to ask where Christ went when He disappeared from their view. Where was He between His appearances during the forty days after His resurrection? Where did He go when He "ascended"? Was He commuting between earth and heaven? Where is He now? Is He near at hand, or biding His time in some distant "heaven"?

The New Testament claims that Jesus ascended to sit "at the right hand of God." That is what Peter said on Pentecost Sunday. Stephen saw Him there and his observation became a keystone of the gospel. Paul writes about it a number of times. In Romans 8, for example, he says, "Who is he that condemns? Christ Jesus, who died—more than that, who was raised to life—is at the right hand of God and is also interceding for us." There is one of the tremendous advantages of Jesus' ascension. We have a friend and intercessor in the very presence of God; Jesus is there, pleading our cause before the throne of grace.

But what does it mean that Jesus is "at the right hand of God?" And when did Jesus go there? Was it only after the ascension? Where was He during those forty days after the resurrection when He wasn't in the presence of His followers? Was He hanging around in some in-between state? Or, did His resurrection place Him immediately at the right hand of God? You will recall that Jesus said to the penitent thief on the cross, "Today you shall be with me in paradise." But you might also recall that He said to Mary of Magdala, "Do not hold on to me, for I have not yet returned to the Father." So where was He? How can we understand where He is now?

Throughout the New Testament, the resurrection and exaltation to the right hand of God are treated together. Accounts of the resurrection typically flow immediately to His exaltation at the right hand of God.

When you put all of these accounts together, it seems that two things are true. First, in accepting a bodily form, Jesus limited

Himself in space and time. When His physical body was in one place, it could not be in another place at the same time. When He walked with His disciples, He was there in Palestine; He was not in heaven and He was not in Athens or Rome or anywhere else at that moment.

On the other hand, now He is apparently able to pass into the presence of God (or into our presence) at any moment. While Jesus clearly treats heaven as a "place"—remember that well-known phrase from John 14, "I go to prepare a place for you"—it is not some distant planet, nor must it be removed from the earth at the edge of the universe. Heaven must be in a different dimension, of which we know next to nothing. But we begin to see, from the experience of Christ, that it is close at hand. Periodically in the Scriptures a person's eyes are opened and he sees this spiritual world, as Stephen did when he saw Jesus standing at the right hand of God. This gives special meaning to Jesus' promise at the end of the Great Commission: "Lo, I am with you always." He truly is with us. He is able to observe what we are doing, to participate in what we are doing, but in a dimension that is not yet revealed to our eyes.

We always picture the ascension as Jesus kind of floating off into space, or perhaps lifting off the earth like the launch of a space shuttle. This has often been ridiculed as a silly, pre-Copernican view of the universe, with heaven somewhere up above the sky in a two- or three-story universe. In fact, however, the word *ascend* is not even used in descriptions of the event. Where it is used later on, it has the connotation of exaltation, as when someone "ascends to the throne," rather than when someone climbs onto an escalator.

What the disciples actually saw was a cloud which hid Him from their sight as He was "taken up" before their very eyes. Again, we say "taken up" (doesn't that mean boosted up into the air?) and hidden by a cloud. I don't think this is likely to be a cumulus cloud into which He disappeared, like a 737 climbing to 30,000 feet. Much more likely, the experience resembled that on the Mount of Transfiguration, where Matthew tells us,

> While he was still speaking, a bright cloud enveloped them, and a voice from the cloud said, "This is my Son, whom I love; with him I am well pleased. Listen to him!" (Matthew 3:17).

The cloud is likely the shekinah glory—the cloud which marked God's presence with His people in the wilderness. And here, as on the Mount of Transfiguration, it simply envelops or embraces Jesus. The word translated *taken up (analambano)* at the beginning and end of this account means variously "to receive up," "to take with," or even "to take on board." It is exactly the same word used when a ship stopped to pick up the apostle Paul on one of his missionary journeys. It does not mean to launch or to send flying off into the air. A second word translated *taken up* in this passage means "to exalt."

It appears that the disciples became aware, as they stood on the mountain outside of Jerusalem, that God the Father had embraced Jesus and removed Him from their view, and in so doing had exalted Him to His own right hand. As the cloud faded, they stood there transfixed, looking at the place in the sky where it had been, until two angels suddenly appeared and addressed them. They assured them that there would ultimately come a day when this Jesus would reappear "in the same way you have seen him go into heaven." Our eyes will be opened and we will see Him returning in our midst.

They had already heard from Jesus that when this happens, it will be in power and great glory, to judge the earth and establish His kingdom for ever and ever. So the disciples, reassured by what they had seen, returned to Jerusalem, excited and joyful, to await this mysterious gift of the Holy Spirit. They were reassured that their Lord, who had begun such an extraordinary work on the earth, was indeed with them. He was going to accompany them, guide them, and protect them. He was going to equip them and encourage them as they carried out His great commission, person-to-person, calling individuals to repentance and discipleship, until Jesus returned to receive His kingship.

From that moment forward we do not find the same kind of fear and hesitation that we found before. The disciples were always confident in Jesus' presence; they were fearful when they thought He was going away. At the ascension, somehow they were reassured that He was going to walk with them and bring to them an added dimension of His presence.

In going away, Jesus could be with them in a more all-encompassing way. Jesus' ascension made it possible for Him to escape the limitations of one body in a material world; according to Ephesians 4:10, His ascension gave Him the opportunity to "fill all things." We do not know how He does it. Clearly, God's Spirit is a part of it, yet it is a very real and personal thing. It is Jesus who walks with us. It is Jesus who walked with His disciples and who has walked with His followers from that day to this.

The fact is, there is great advantage in Jesus being with us in such a form. We don't need to wait in line for His attention. We don't need to make an appointment to spend a half-hour talking with Him while everyone else awaits their turn. We who follow Jesus are never alone. Though He is in only one place when He appears in bodily form, He "fills all things" when He is in the presence of the Father. In our darkest night, in our most difficult trial, in our most challenging assignment, Jesus truly is walking beside us.

Every Christian has this assurance. We may need to have a heart, ears, eyes, and minds that are tuned to experience the presence of Jesus Christ with us, but in His ascension, we are assured of His intercession for us at the right hand of God, His promise to "fill all things," and His commitment to accompany us "even to the very end of the age."

Epilogue

So what do you think, now that you have met the most incredible man who ever lived and walked with Him through the most astonishing events of history? At the risk of understatement, may I suggest that to meet such a man must inevitably change the course of our lives?

We have only two options, really. We may turn and walk away, unwilling to believe our eyes and ears (or the eyes and ears of those who were there). We may say that such a thing as God visiting our planet is impossible to accept (though I must say such a prejudice is hopelessly provincial). If this is our choice, we must live out our lives with no hope of knowing God, no certain model of how we should live, and no hope of life beyond the grave.

But we may also respond as did those who were closest to Jesus. The more closely they looked at Jesus, the more they became convinced that He truly was who He claimed to be. We may make our own judgment, based upon our own encounter with this man. Convinced by His astonishing authority, His revealing miracles, and His compelling lifestyle, we also may accept Him for who He claimed to be.

If we, like his original followers, embrace Him as Lord, it must make all the difference in the world to us, as it did to them. Like them, we will feel compelled to become His disciples. Like them, we will pursue every opportunity to get to know Him more personally. Like them, we will find it impossible to refrain from trying to convince everyone we know. For if God has walked into our lives in the person of Jesus, nothing can ever be the same. Our wildest hopes have just become possible!

Bibliography

Aharoni, Yohanan and Michael Avi-Yonah. Prepared by Carta, Ltd. *The MacMillan Bible Atlas*. New York: MacMillan Publishing Co., Inc., 1968.

Alexander, David and Pat, ed. *Eerdmans' Handbook to the Bible*. Grand Rapids, Mich.: William B. Eerdmans Publishing, 1973.

Barclay, William. *The Gospel of John*. Vol. 2. Philadelphia: The Westminster Press, 1956.

Barclay, William. *The Gospel of Luke*. Phildelphia: The Westminster Press, 1956.

Barclay, William. *The Gospel of Mark*. Phildelphia: The Westminster Press, 1956.

Barclay, William. *The Gospel of Matthew*. Vol. 2. Philadelphia: The Westminster Press, 1958.

Bornkamm, Gunther. *Jesus of Nazareth*. Translated by Irene and Fraser McLuskey. New York: Harper & Row, 1960.

Bruce, F.F. *New Testament History*. Garden City, N.Y.: Doubleday & Company, Inc., 1969.

Bruce, F.F. *Jesus and Paul: Places They Knew*. Nashville: Thomas Nelson, Inc., 1981.

Chesterton, Gilbert K. *Orthodoxy.* Garden City, N.Y.: Image Books, 1936.

Clark, Dennis E. *The Life and Teaching of Jesus the Messiah.* Elgin, Ill.: Dove Publications, 1977.

Edersheim, Alfred. *The Life and Times of Jesus the Messiah.* Vol. 2. McLean, Virginia: MacDonald Publishing Company, DATE.

Edwards, William D., Wesley J. Gabel, Floyd E. Hosmer, "On the Physical Death of Jesus Christ." *Journal of the American Medical Association* (March 21, 1986): 1455-1463.

Foster, Richard. *Celebration of Discipline: The Path to Spiritual Growth.* San Francisco: Harper & Row, 1978.

Gilbert, Douglas and Clyde S. Kilby. *C.S. Lewis: Images of His World.* Grand Rapids, Mich.: William. B. Eerdmans Publishing Company, 1973.

Gower, Ralph. *The New Manners and Customs of Bible Times.* Chicago, Ill: Moody Press, 1987.

Hendriksen, William. *New Testament Commentary: Exposition of the Gospel According to Luke.* Grand Rapids, Mich.: Baker Book House, 1978.

Hendriksen, William. *New Testament Commentary: Exposition of the Gospel According to Matthew.* Grand Rapids, Mich.: Baker Book House, 1973.

Jeremias, Joachim. *Jerusalem in the Time of Jesus.* Translated by F.H. and C.H. Cave. Philadelphia: Fortress Press, 1969.

Lane, William L. *The Gospel According to Mark,* Grand Rapids, Mich.: William. B. Eerdmans Publishing Company, 1974.

Lewis, C.S. *Mere Christianity.* New York: The Macmillan Company, 1952.

Lewis, C.S. *Miracles: A Preliminary Study.* New York: The Macmillan Company, 1947.

Lewis, C.S. *The Screwtape Letters and Screwtape Proposes a Toast.* New York: Macmillan, 1959.

MacDonald, Gordon. *The Effective Father.* Wheaton, Ill.: Tyndale House Publishers, Inc., 1977.

Maier, Paul L. *First Christmas: The True and Unfamiliar Story in Words and Pictures.* New York: Harper & Row, 1971.

Morris, Leon. *The Gospel According To John.* Grand Rapids, Mich.: William. B. Eerdmans Publishing Company, 1973.

Morris, Leon. *The Lord From Heaven.* Grand Rapids, Michigan: Wm. B. Eerdmans Publishing Company, 1958.

National Geographic Society. *Everyday Life in Bible Times.* A volume in the Story of Man Library prepared by National Geographic Book Service, 1967.

Packer, J.I. *Knowing God.* Downers Grove, Ill.: InterVarsity Press, 1973.

Peck, M. Scott. *The People of the Lie.* New York: Simon and Schuster, 1983.

Rogerson, John. *Atlas of the Bible.* New York: Facts on File, 1985.

Shaw, Luci. "YES to Shame and Glory." *Christianity Today* (December 12, 1986): 22-24.

Stauffer, Ethelbert. *Jesus and His Story.* Translated by Richard and Clara Winston. New York: Alfred A. Knopf, 1959.

Stott, John R. W. *Basic Christianity.* Grand Rapids, Mich.: Williamm. B. Eerdmans Publishing Company, 1958.

Tenney, Merrill C. *New Testament Survey.* Grand Rapids, Mich.: William. B. Eerdmans Publishing Co., Inc., 1961.

Thompson, J.A. *Handbook of Life In Bible Times.* Downers Grove, Ill.: Inter-Varsity Press, 1986.

Wallace, Lew. *Ben Hur: A Tale of the Christ.* New York: Harper & Brothers, 1880.

Willard, Dallas. *The Spirit of the Disciplines: Understanding How God Changes Lives.* San Francisco: Harper & Row, 1988.

Wise, Robert L. *When There Is No Miracle.* Glendale, Calif.: Regal Books, 1977.